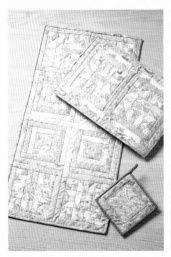

January – Snowflakes
Aviary by 3 Sisters
page 4

February – Hearts
Wonderland by MoMo
page 5

March – Flowers
Patisserie by Fig Tree Quilts
page 6

April – Baskets
Sweet by Urban Chiks
page 7

May – Favorite Things
Hello Betty by Chloe's Closet
page 8

June – Flower Garden
Soiree by Lila Tueller
page 9

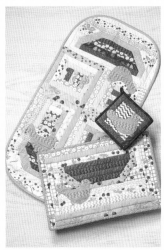

July – Picnic
Oh Cherry Oh by Me & My Sister
page 10

August – Homestead
Legacy by Howard Marcus
page 11

September – On the Farm
Flag Day Farm
by Minick & Simpson
page 12

October – Pumpkins
Fresh by Deb Strain
page 13

November – at Home
Wildflower Serenade II
by Kansas Troubles
page 14

December – Holiday Favorites
Harmony by Jan Patek
page 15

January – Snowflakes

pieced & quilted by Donna Arends Hansen
Capture the beauty of snowflakes... one of Winter's most
spectacular creations with a collection of frosty snowflakes
that will warm up your seasonal decor.

FABRIC USED: "Aviary" by 3 Sisters
instructions on pages 23 - 26

February – Hearts

pieced & quilted by Rose Ann Pegram
*Brighten a Winter afternoon with a cheerful bit of sewing
that will fill your breakfast room or kitchen with traditional sym-
bols of love. Quick techniques allow you to easily piece these
happy hearts in a fabulous collection of practical projects...great
for your home and whenever you need a heartfelt gift.*

FABRIC USED: "Wonderland" by MoMo

instructions on pages 27 - 30

March – Flowers

pieced and quilted by Janice Irick
There is nothing like early Spring flowers to shake off the chill
of Winter. This March you can ignore the frost outside as Poppies
and Tulips bloom from your sewing room to your kitchen.

FABRIC USED: "Patisserie" by Fig Tree Quilts
instructions on pages 31 - 34

April – Baskets

pieced and quilted by Janice Irick

'Tis the season for a fresh look! Soften the spaces in your home with gentle pastels that whisper hints of the coming Spring. Break away from the harsh Winter months with this light and breezy collection.

FABRIC USED: "Sweet" by Urban Chiks

instructions on pages 35 - 38

May – My Favorite Things

pieced and quilted by Rose Ann Pegram
Mix and match your favorite motifs with this fabulous sampler.
Whether you love houses, pets, or nature, you will find a design to
please. Coordinate your creativity with the style of your home.

FABRIC USED: "Hello Betty" by Chloe's Closet
instructions on pages 39 - 44

June – Flower Garden

pieced and quilted by Donna Perrotta
*Every gardener's delight! Beautiful flowers have been used
over the ages to celebrate every heartfelt sentiment from devoted
love to Congratulations and Happy Birthday. Share the joys of
flowers when you set your table with this cheerful fabric collection.*

FABRIC USED: "Soiree" by LilaTueller
instructions on pages 45 - 48

July – Picnic

*pieced and quilted by Rose Ann Pegram
and Edna Summers*

*Cheery colors brighten your decor as beautifully as the Summer
sun beaming through sparkling windows. Welcome your guests to a
festive table with delicious watermelon motifs.*

FABRIC USED: "Oh Cherry Oh" by Me & My Sister
instructions on pages 49 - 52

August- Homestead

You can feel Autumn on the breeze. Mix warm reds and blues with soft earth tones for a natural complement to your seasonal decor.

FABRIC USED: "Legacy" by Howard Marcus
instructions on pages 53 - 57

September – On the Farm

pieced and quilted by Lanelle Herron
Create a patriotic theme that complements your decor all year
round. Half-square triangles make this intriguing design easy to construct.

FABRIC USED: "Flag Day Farm" by Minick & Simpson
instructions on pages 58 - 59

October – Pumpkins

pieced and quilted by Donna Perrotta
Have a frightfully fun harvest celebration with friendly seasonal motifs. Cheery Jack-o-Lanterns, candy corns and kitty cats adorn this fabulous holiday collection.

FABRIC USED: "Fresh" by Deb Strain
instructions on pages 60 - 63

November – at Home

pieced & quilted by Donna Perrotta
Family gatherings are wonderful times for love and sharing.
Make your holidays even more special with memorable table
decor that celebrates hearth and home.

FABRIC USED: "Wildflower Serenade II" by Kansas Troubles
instructions on pages 64 - 67

December – Favorite Things

pieced and quilted by Rose Ann Pegram
Welcome friends and family to your holiday table with a
delightful sampling of seasonal motifs. Eight easy blocks bring to
mind the joys of sharing hearth and home with those you love.
These blocks would make a lovely sampler baby quilt too!

FABRIC USED: "Harmony" by Jan Patek
instructions on pages 72 - 82

Harmony Quilt

pieced by Donna Kinsey, quilted by Sue Needle

Small blocks are fun to make because several can be pieced easily in an afternoon. Each block can make a charming potholder. You can easily expand your creativity to include larger projects using the small blocks.

Small blocks make wonderful quilts, and setting them on point allows you to make a large quilt with fewer blocks.

FABRIC USED: Harmony" by Jan Patek (see page 15)

instructions on pages 17 - 22

Harmony Quilt

photo on pages 16 and 83

SIZE: Quilt: 52" x 61"
       Potholder: 7" x 7"

YARDAGE:
We used a *Moda* "Harmony" by Jan Patek
    'Honey Bun' collection of 1½" fabric strips
    - we purchased 1 'Honey Bun'

7 strips	OR	⅓ yard Red
6 strips	OR	¼ yard Green
6 strips	OR	¼ yard Tan
5 strips	OR	¼ yard Black
4 strips	OR	⅙ yard Light Brown
2 strips	OR	⅛ yard Blue
2 strips	OR	⅛ yard Paisley

Alternate blocks & Side triangles	Purchase 1⅛ yards Black tiny print #1
Border #1	Purchase ⅜ yard Black small print #2
Border #2	Purchase ⅜ yard Tan print
Border #3 & Binding	Purchase 1⅝ yards Black medium print #3
Backing	Purchase 3 yards
Batting	Purchase 60" x 69"
Sewing machine, needle, thread	

FABRIC FOR INDIVIDUAL PROJECTS:
Scraps for the Potholder:

1 strip	OR	1½" x 44" of each color
Binding	Purchase	2½" x 44"
Backing	Purchase	9" x 9"
Batting	Purchase	9" x 9"

PREPARATION FOR STRIPS:
    Cut all strips 1½" by the width of fabric (usually 42" - 44").
    Label the stacks or pieces as you cut.

SEW BLOCKS:
    Refer to the Cutting Chart and Assembly instructions for
        each block.
    Label the pieces as you cut.

YARDAGE CUTTING CHART:
    Cut the following from Black tiny print #1 yardage to set
between the pieced blocks.
    This makes a beautiful setting to show off your blocks.

Quantity	Length	Position
Cut from Yardage:		
12	7½" x 7½"	A - Alternate blocks
4	11½" x 11½"	B - Border triangles
2	6½" x 6½"	C - Corner triangles

For A - Alternate Blocks, leave each block square.

PREPARATION FOR TRIANGLES:

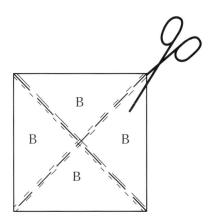

For B - Border Triangles, draw 2 diagonal lines on each 11½" square.
    Stay stitch on each side of both diagonals with a ⅛" seam to prevent triangles from stretching on the bias. This is an important step.
    Cut on the diagonal lines.
    Label the Border Triangles "B".

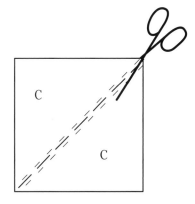

For C - Corner Triangles, draw 1 diagonal line on each 6½" square.
    Stay stitch on each side of the diagonal with a ⅛" seam to prevent triangles from stretching on the bias.
    Cut on the diagonal line.
    Label the Corner Triangles "C".

Harmony Quilt - Border Assembly

ASSEMBLY:
Make 20 pieced blocks (see pages 20 - 22).
Arrange all pieced blocks and all A - Alternate blocks and
    B - Corner blocks on a work surface or table.
Refer to the border assembly diagram for block placement.
Sew the diagonal rows together. Press.
Sew C - Corner triangles to the corners of the quilt. Press.

BORDERS:
Note - Irrational Fractions:
    Because the length of the diagonal on Border squares is an
irrational number, the length of the quilt will have to be an
unusual fraction.
    To avoid this problem, we have given you a little extra
length on the borders.
    You will trim each border to fit.

Note - Perfect Border Lengths:
    Side strips will be the same length as the center of quilt.
    Carefully lay both strips down the center of quilt. Pin
them to be sure they lay flat with no waves. When you are
satisfied that they are laying flat, mark or cut off the excess
length. Now you can move each side to its side of the quilt.
    Carefully align each border strip with its side, pin in place.
    TIP: I begin pinning at each end of a strip then work
out any small waves along the center of the strip.

Border #1:
Cut strips 1½" by the width of fabric.
Sew strips together end to end.
    Cut 2 strips 1½" x 54" for sides.
    Cut 2 strips 1½" x 44" for top and bottom.
    Sew top and bottom borders to the quilt. Press.
    Sew side borders to the quilt. Press.
Border #2:
Cut strips 1½" by the width of fabric.
Sew strips together end to end.
    Cut 2 strips 1½" x 54" for sides.
    Cut 2 strips 1½" x 46" for top and bottom.
    Sew side borders to the quilt. Press.
    Sew top and bottom borders to the quilt. Press.
Border #3:
Cut strips 4½" wide parallel to the selvage to
    eliminate piecing.
    Cut 2 strips 4½" x 56" for sides.
    Cut 2 strips 4½" x 53" for top and bottom.
    Sew side borders to the quilt. Press.
    Sew top and bottom borders to the quilt. Press.

FINISHING:
Quilting: See Basic Instructions.
Binding: Cut strips 2½" wide.
        Sew together end to end to equal 236".
        See Binding Instructions.

Harmony Quilt - Assembly Diagram

Cutting:

Color	Quantity - Length			
Red	1 - 3½"	1 - 5½"		
Light Brown	2 - 1½"	1 - 3½"	1 - 2½"	1 - 5½"
Blue	1 - 2½"	1 - 1½"		
Tan	2 - 1½"	1 - 5½"	2 - 6½"	1 - 7½"

Assembly: Refer to the Potholder diagram.

Roof section: Sew #1-2-3. Press.
Sew #4 & 5 to the bottom and top of 1-2-3. Press.

House section: Sew #6-7-8. Press.
Sew #9 to the bottom of 6-7-8. Press.
Sew #10 & 11 to the left side of the piece. Press.
Sew #12 to the top of the piece. Press.
Sew the roof section to the house. Press.
Sew #13 & 14 to the left and right sides of the block. Press.
Sew #15 to the bottom of the block. Press.

Quilting: See Basic Instructions.
Binding: Cut a strip 2½" x 42". See Binding Instructions.
Add a loop to the upper left corner if desired.

Potholder   photo on page 16

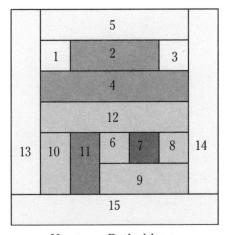

Harmony Potholder

Chart 1 - Block 1:

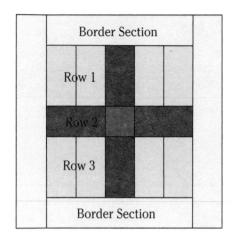

For 3 Blocks, cut the Lengths for Strips:

All cut strips are 1½" by the measurement given.

Color	Quantity - Length
Green	4 - 15"
Black	1 - 15"
Black	6 - 2½"
Blue	3 - 1½"
Tan	6 - 7½"
Tan	6 - 5½"

Rows 1 & 3: Sew the following 15" strips to make a piece 5½" x 15":
Green - Green - Black - Green - Green. Press.
Cut the piece into 6 sections, each 2½" x 5½".

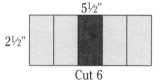

Row 2: Sew Black - Blue - Black. Press. Make 3.
Sew the rows together. Press.
Sew the top and bottom Tan borders to the block. Press.
Sew the side borders to the block. Press.

Chart 2 - Block 2:

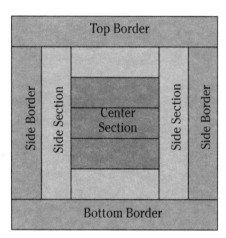

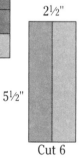

For 3 Blocks, cut the Lengths for Strips:

All cut strips are 1½" by the measurement given.

Color	Quantity - Length	
Red	3 - 10½"	
Light Brown	2 - 10½"	1 - 33"
Paisley	1 - 33"	6 - 7½"

Center section: Sew the following 11" strips to make a piece 5½" x 11":
Lt Brown - 3 Red - Lt Brown. Press.
Cut the piece into 3 sections 3½" x 5½".
Side sections: Sew the following 33" strips to make a piece 2½" x 33": Lt Brown - Paisley. Press.
Cut the piece into 6 sections 2½" x 5½".
Sew a Side section to the right and left of each center. Press.
Sew the 7½" Paisley borders to the top and bottom. Press.

Chart 3 - Block 3:

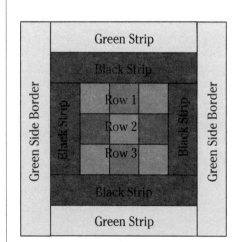

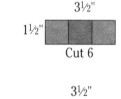

For 3 Blocks, cut the Lengths for Strips:

All cut strips are 1½" by the measurement given.

Color	Quantity - Length	
Red	1 - 9"	2 - 5"
Blue	2 - 9"	1 - 5"
Black	1 - 33"	6 - 3½"
Green	1 - 33"	6 - 7½"

Checkerboard:
Rows 1 & 3: Sew the following 9½" strips to make a piece 3½" x 9": Blue - Red - Blue. Press.
Cut the piece into 6 sections 1½" x 3½".
Row 2: Sew the following 5" strips to make a piece 3½" x 5":
Red - Blue - Red. Press.
Cut the piece into 3 sections 1½" x 3½".

Sew the rows together. Press. Make 3.
Sew a Black 3½" strip to the right and left sides of each checkerboard. Press.
Top & Bottom Borders: Sew the Black and Green 33" strips together to make a piece 2½" x 33". Press.
Cut the piece into 6 sections 2½" x 5½".
Sew a section to the top and bottom of each checkerboard. Press.
Sew the Green side borders to each block. Press.

Chart 4 - Block 4:

For 3 Blocks, cut the Lengths for Strips:
All cut strips are 1½" by the measurement given.

Color	Quantity - Length		
Red	2 - 9"	1 - 33"	6 - 3½"
Blue	1 - 9"	3 - 3½"	
Green	6 - 7½"	1 - 33"	

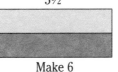

3½"
1½"
Cut 6

Rows 1 & 3: Sew the following 9" strips to make a piece 3½" x 9": Red - Blue - Red. Press. Cut the piece into 6 sections, each 1½" x 3½".

Center section: Sew a Checkerboard row to the top and bottom of each Blue 3½" strip. Press. Sew a Red 3½" strip to the right and left sides of each center section. Press.

Top & Bottom Borders: Sew the Red and Green 33" strips together to make a piece 2½" x 33". Press.
Cut the piece into 6 sections 2½" x 5½".
Sew a section to the top and bottom of each center. Press.
Sew a Green border to the left and right sides of each block. Press.

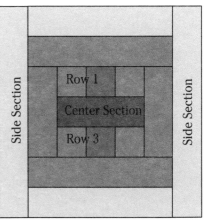

5½"
3½"
Make 3

5½"
2½"
Make 6

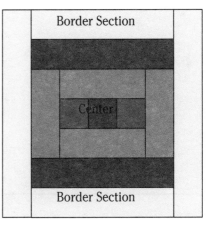

Block 4 - Assembly

Row 1
Center Section
Row 3
Side Section / Side Section

Chart 6 - Block 6:

For 3 Blocks, cut the Lengths for Strips:
All cut strips are 1½" by the measurement given.

Color	Quantity - Length	
Blue	2 - 4½"	
Black	1 - 33"	1 - 4½"
Tan	1 - 33"	6 - 7½"
Red	12 - 3½"	

3½"
1½"
Cut 3

Center: Sew the following 4½" strips to make a piece 3½" x 4½": Blue - Black - Blue. Press.
Cut the piece into 3 sections 1½" x 3½".
Sew a Red 3½" strip to the top and bottom of each Center. Press. Make 3.
Sew a Red 3½" strip to the right and left sides of each Center. Press.

Top/Bottom Borders: Sew the Black and Tan 33" strips together to make a piece 2½" x 33". Press.
Cut the piece into 6 sections 2½" x 5½".
Sew a section to the top and bottom of each center. Press.
Sew a Tan border to the left and right sides of each block. Press.

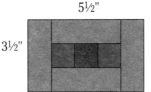

5½"
3½"
Make 3

5½"
2½"
Make 6

Border Section
Center
Border Section

Block 6 - Assembly Diagram

Chart 7 - Block 7:

TIP: Make this block last and use all your scraps.
For 3 Blocks, cut the Lengths for Strips:
All cut strips are 1½" by the measurement given.

Color	Quantity - Length			
Light Brown	6 - 7½"	6 - 5½"		
Red	3 - 5½"	3 - 4½"	3 - 3½"	3 - 2½"
Green	3 - 4½"	3 - 3½"		
Blue	3 - 2½"	3 - 1½"		
Black	3 - 1½"			

2½"
2½"
3
2 1
Make 3

Sew 1 to 2, then sew 3 to 1-2.
Sew additional strips in numerical sequence, add 4, then 5, 6, 7, 8, 9, 10, 11, 12 and 13 to make the Log Cabin block. Press.

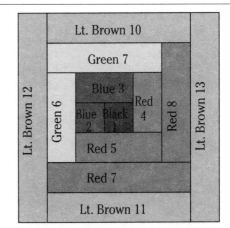

Lt. Brown 10
Green 7
Blue 3
Blue 2 | Black 1 | Red 4
Red 5
Red 7
Lt. Brown 11
Lt. Brown 12 / Green 6 / Red 8 / Lt. Brown 13

Block 7 - Assembly Diagram

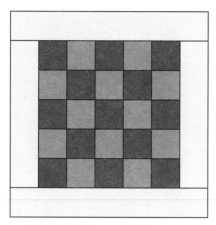

Block 5 - Assembly Diagram

Chart 5 - Block 5:
For 2 Blocks, cut the Lengths for Strips:
All cut strips are 1½" by the measurement given.

	Quantity	Length	Position
Red	2	9"	Section A
	3	6"	Section B
Black	3	9"	Section A
	2	6"	Section B
Tan	4	7½"	Top and Bottom borders
	4	5½"	Side borders

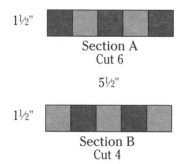

5½"

1½"

Section A
Cut 6

5½"

1½"

Section B
Cut 4

PREPARATION FOR BLOCK 5
Section A for Rows 1, 3 & 5:
Sew 9" strips together side by side to make 5½" x 9":
Black - Red - Black - Red - Black. Press.
Cut this piece into 6 sections 1½" x 5½". Label these "A".

Section B for Rows 2 & 4:
Sew 6" strips together side by side to make 5½" x 6":
Red - Black - Red - Black - Red. Press.
Cut this piece into 4 sections 1½" x 5½". Label these "B".

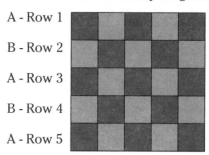

Checkerboard - Assembly Diagram

A - Row 1
B - Row 2
A - Row 3
B - Row 4
A - Row 5

Checkerboard:
Arrange the rows in the following order:
A - B - A - B - A.
Sew the rows together. Press.

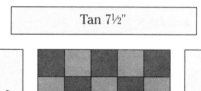

Tan 7½"

Tan 5½"

Tan

Tan

Block 5 - Assembly Diagram

BLOCK ASSEMBLY:
Refer to the Block Assembly diagram.
Sew Tan 5½" strips to the right and left
sides of block. Press.
Sew Tan 7½" strips to the top and
bottom of block. Press.

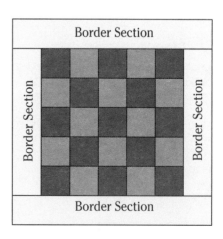

Border Section

Border Section

Border Section

Border Section

January – Snowflakes

photo on page 4

SIZE: Table Runner: 18" x 36"
           Placemat: 13" x 20"
           Potholder: 7" x 7"

YARDAGE:

We used a *Moda* "Aviary" by 3 Sisters 'Honey Bun' collection of 1½" fabric strips - we purchased 1 'Honey Bun'

11 strips	OR	½ yard White
9 strips	OR	⅜ yard Aqua
7 strips	OR	⅓ yard Green
5 strips	OR	¼ yard Pink

Binding	Purchase ⅝ yard
Backing	Purchase 1 yard
Batting	Purchase 36" x 38"

Sewing machine, needle, thread

FABRIC FOR INDIVIDUAL PROJECTS:

Fabric or Scraps for Table Runner:

8 strips	OR	12" x 44" of White (⅓ yard)
7 strips	OR	10½" x 44" of Aqua (⅓ yard)
5 strips	OR	7½" x 44" of Green (¼ yard)
3 strips	OR	4½" x 44" of Pink (⅛ yard)
Binding	Purchase 2½" x 118" (¼ yard)
Backing	Purchase ⅝ yard
Batting	Purchase 20" x 38"

Fabric or Scraps for Placemat:

3 strips	OR	4½" x 44" of Aqua (⅛ yard)
3 strips	OR	4½" x 44" of White (⅛ yard)
2 strips	OR	3" x 44" of Green
2 strips	OR	3" x 44" of Pink
Binding	Purchase 2½" x 76" (⅙ yard)
Backing	Purchase 15" x 22"
Batting	Purchase 15" x 22"

Scraps for Each Potholder:

1 strip	OR	1½" x 44" of each color
Applique	1½" x 22" of White
Binding	Purchase 2½" x 44" (⅛ yard)
Backing	Purchase 9" x 9"
Batting	Purchase 9" x 9"

PREPARATION FOR STRIPS:

Cut all strips 1½" by the width of fabric (usually 42" - 44").

Snowball Corners

Several strips in each block use the Snowball Corner technique. The direction of the diagonal for each strip in the block varies, so you must carefully note the diagonal on the block assembly diagram. Some strips have a corner on only one end. The squares used as Corners are labelled with a "c" in the cutting list.

TIP: Fold back the triangle and check its position before you sew.

STEPS: Align a square with the appropriate end of the strip and sew on the diagonal line. Fold the triangle back, press before attaching it to any other strips.

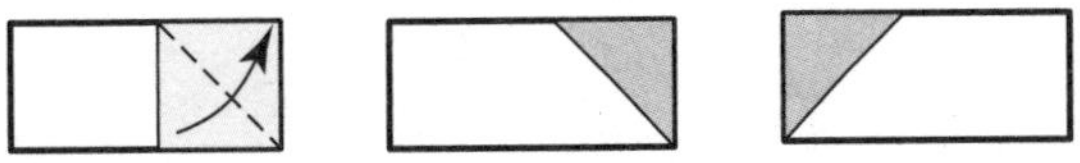

SECTIONS AND UNITS FOR BLOCKS 1 & 2:

Section A:

Make 24 of Unit 1 and 24 of Unit 2.

Unit 1:

Cut 1 White and 1 Aqua strip 36½".
Sew the strips together to make a piece 2½" x 36½". Press.
Cut 24 sections 1½" x 2½".
Label them Unit 1.

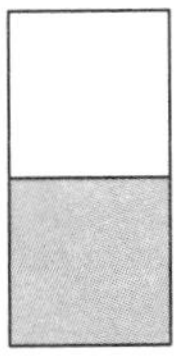

Unit 1 Cut 24

Unit 2:

Cut 48 "c" Aqua squares 1½" x 1½".
Cut 24 White pieces 1½" x 1¾".
Match 24 Aqua and 24 White pieces.
Draw 1 diagonal line and sew a Snowball Corner onto each White piece with an Aqua square.
Fold back the Aqua triangle and press.
This square will look like a half-square triangle, but it will remain 1½" x 1½".
Do NOT use the Half-Square Triangles technique because the block will be too small.
Refer to the Unit 2 diagram and sew an Aqua square to each white/Aqua Snowball square. Press.

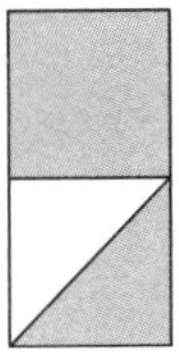

Unit 2 Make 24

Section A:

Make 24 of Section A.
Refer to the Section A diagram.
Sew Unit 1 to Unit 2. Press.
Make 24.

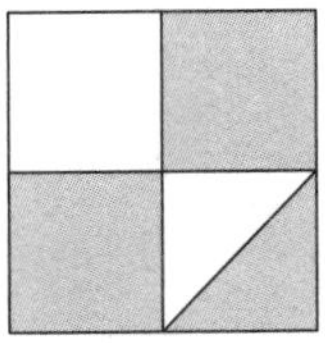

Section A - Make 24

Section B:

Make 24 of Column 1,
    24 of Column 2 and
    24 of Column 3.
Make 8 "Y" blocks
Refer to the Section B diagram.

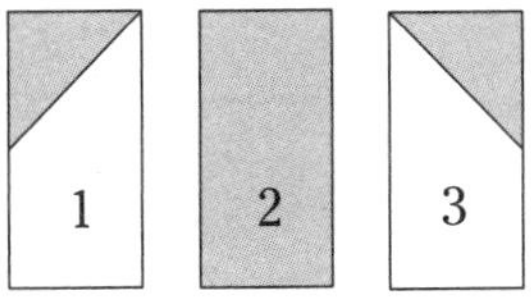

Make 24 of each column (1, 2 & 3).

Cut pieces:
Cut 48 Aqua "c" 1½" x 1½" squares
#1 - Cut 24 White 1½" x 2½" strips.
#3 - Cut 24 White 1½" x 2½" strips.
#2 - Cut 24 Aqua 1½" x 2½" strips.

Sew pieces:
Align 1 Aqua "c" 1½" x 1½" square on #1 White.
Align 1 Aqua "c" 1½" x 1½" square on #3 White.
Refer to the Snowball Corner instructions.
Sew on the diagonal, fold back the pieces and press.

Sew blocks:
To make the 'T' block, sew 1-2-3. Press. Make 12.
To make the 'Y' block, sew 3-2-1. Press. Make 12.

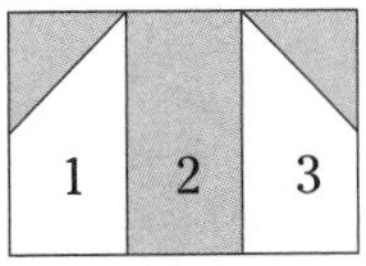

'T' Block - Make 12

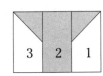

'Y' Block - Make 12

Cut 18 White

Unit 3
Make 12

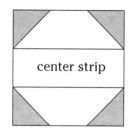

center strip

Section C
Make 6

Section C:

Cut 18 White 3½" x 1½" strips. Save 6 for the centers.

Sew Unit 3:

Cut 24 Aqua "c" 1½" x 1½" squares.
Refer to the Unit 3 diagram.
Align an Aqua "c" 1½" square on each end of a White strip.
Refer to the Snowball Corner instructions.
Sew on the diagonal, fold back the pieces and press.
Make 12.

Sew Section 3:

Refer to the Section C diagram.
Sew a Unit 3 - a 3½" White center strip - a Unit 3. Press.
Make 6.

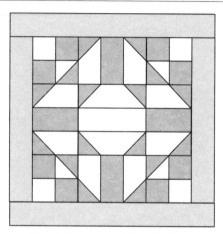

Block 1 - Assembly - Make 3

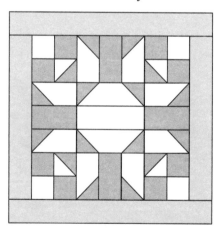

Block 2 - Assembly - Make 3

BLOCK 1:

Rows 1 & 3: Sew Section A - T block - Section A. Press.
Row 2: Sew T block - Section C - T block. Press.
Sew the rows together. Press. Make 3.

BLOCK 2:

Rows 1 & 3: Sew Section A - Y block - Section A. Press.
Row 2: Sew Y block - Section C - Y block. Press.
Sew the rows together. Press. Make 3.

Borders for Blocks 1 & 2:

Cut 12 Green strips 1½" x 7½" for sides.
Cut 12 Green strips 1½" x 9½" for top and bottom.
Sew side borders to each block. Press.
Sew top and bottom borders to each block. Press.

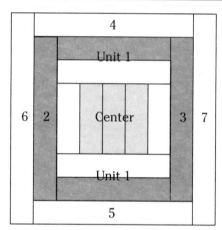

Block 3 - Assembly - Make 4

BLOCK 3:

Center:

Cut 2 White and 3 Green
  strips 1½" x 14".
Sew the strips, White-
  3 Green - White to make
  a piece 5½" x 14".
Cut the piece into 4 sections,
  each 3½" x 5½".

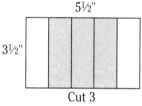

5½"

3½"

Cut 3

Top and Bottom Unit 1 Borders:

Cut 1 Pink and 1 White strip, each 1½" x 11".
Sew the strips together to make a piece 2½" x 11".
Cut the piece into 2 sections, each 2½" x 5½".
Sew a section to the top and bottom of a center.
  Press.
Cut 1 Pink and 1 White strip, each 1½" x 33".
Sew the strips together to make a piece 2½" x 33".
Cut the piece into 6 sections, each 2½" x 5½".
Sew a section to the top and bottom of the center.
  Press.
Make 4

Borders:

#2 & 3: Cut 8 Pink strips 1½" x 7½".
#4 & 5: Cut 4 White and 4 Aqua strips 1½" x 7½".
#6 & 7: Cut 4 White and 4 Aqua strips 1½" x 9½".
Refer to the Block 3 diagram.
Sew #2 & 3 to the left and right sides. Press.
Sew #4 & 5 to the top and bottom. Press.
Sew #6 & 7 to the left and right sides. Press.
Make 4 blocks.

Table Runner

Refer to the Table Runner Assembly diagram.
Arrange all blocks on a work surface or table.

Rows 1 & 4: Sew Block 2 to Block 1. Press.

Rows 2 & 3: Sew 2 of Block 3 together. Press.

Sew the rows together. Press.

Quilting: See Basic Instructions.
Binding: Cut strips 2½" wide.
Sew together end to end to equal 118".
See Binding Instructions.

Snowflake Table Runner Assembly

Placemat

Refer to the Placemat Assembly diagram.
Sew a Block 1 to Block 2. Press.

Border #1:
Cut 2 White strips 1½" x 18½" for top and bottom.
Sew top and bottom borders to the mat. Press.

Border #2:
Cut 2 Pink strips 1½" x 11½" for sides.
Cut 2 Pink strips 1½" x 20½" for top and bottom.
Sew side borders to the mat. Press.
Sew top and bottom borders to the mat. Press.

Quilting: See Basic Instructions.
Binding: Cut strips 2½" wide.
Sew together end to end to equal 76".
See Binding Instructions.

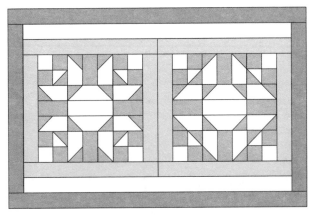

Snowflake Placemat Assembly

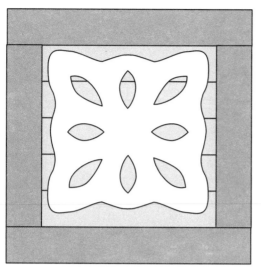

Snowflake Potholder

Snowflake Potholder

Refer to the Potholder Assembly diagram.
Cut 5 Green 5½"strips.
Sew the strips together to make a piece 5½" x 5½".
   Press.

Border:
Cut 2 Pink strips 1½" x 5½" for sides.
Cut 2 Pink strips 1½" x 7½" for top and bottom.
Sew side borders to the potholder. Press.
Sew top and bottom borders to the potholder. Press.

APPLIQUE:
Cut 4 White 5½" strips.
Sew the strips together to make a piece 4½" x 5½".
   Press.
Use this piece to cut out the snowflake applique.
Refer to the Applique Instructions.
Applique as desired.

Quilting: See Basic Instructions.
Binding: Cut strips 2½" wide.
   Sew together end to end to equal 38".
   See Binding Instructions.

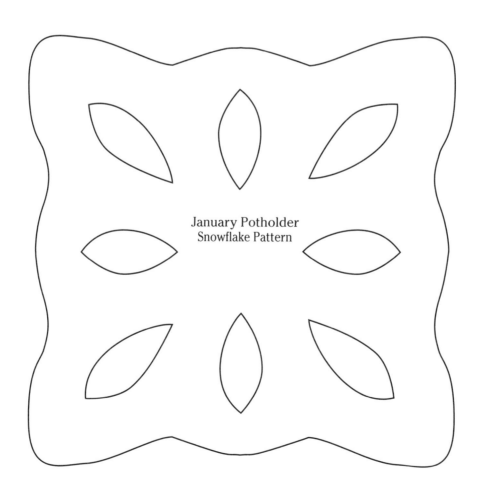

January Potholder
Snowflake Pattern

February – Hearts

photo on page 5

SIZE: Table Runner: 14" x 36"
       Placemat: 10" x 14"
       Potholders: 8" x 8"

YARDAGE:
We used a *Moda* "Wonderland" by MoMo
   'Honey Bun' collection of 1½" fabric strips
   - we purchased 1 'Honey Bun'

10 strips	OR	½ yard Ivory
5 strips	OR	¼ yard Red
4 strips	OR	⅙ yard Green
2 strips	OR	⅛ yard Brown
1 strip	OR	⅛ yard Aqua
1 strip	OR	⅛ yard Blue

Binding   Purchase ⅝ yard
Backing   Purchase ¾ yard
Batting   Purchase 36" x 38"
Sewing machine, needle, thread

FABRIC FOR INDIVIDUAL PROJECTS:
Fabric or Scraps for Table Runner:

6 strips	OR	9" x 44" of Ivory (¼ yard)
3 strips	OR	4½" x 44" of Green (⅛ yard)
3 strips	OR	4½" x 44" of Red (⅛ yard)
1 strip	OR	1½" x 44" of Aqua
1 strip	OR	1½" x 44" of Blue

Binding   Purchase 2½" x 96" (¼ yard)
Backing   Purchase ½ yard
Batting   Purchase 16" x 38"

Fabric or Scraps for Placemat:

2 strips	OR	3" x 44" of Ivory
2 strips	OR	3" x 44" of Brown
1 strip	OR	1½" x 44" of Green
1 strip	OR	1½" x 44" of Red

Binding   Purchase 2½" x 58"
Backing   Purchase 12" x 16"
Batting   Purchase 12" x 16"

Scraps for Each Potholder:

1 strip	OR	1½" x 44" of each color
Applique		1½" x 12" of Red

Binding   Purchase 2½" x 44" (⅛ yard)
Backing   Purchase 9" x 9"
Batting   Purchase 9" x 9"

PREPARATION FOR STRIPS:
   Cut all strips 1½" by the width of fabric (usually 42" - 44").

SEW BLOCKS:
   Refer to the Cutting Chart and Assembly instructions for each block.
   TIP: For each block, cut pieces "c", 2, 6, 7, 8, 9, & 10 from the same Ivory strip. Label the pieces as you cut.

Snowball Corners

Several strips in each block use the Snowball Corner technique. The direction of the diagonal for each strip in the block varies, so you must carefully note the diagonal on the block assembly diagram. Some strips have a corner on only one end. The squares used as Corners are labelled with a "c" in the cutting list.

   TIP: Fold back the triangle and check its position before you sew.

   STEPS: Align a square with the appropriate end of the strip and sew on the diagonal line. Fold the triangle back, press before attaching it to any other strips.

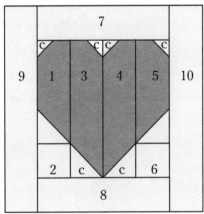

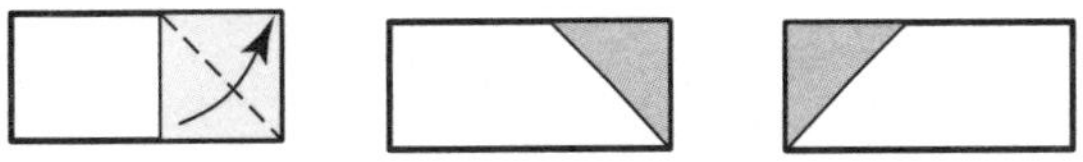

Block A

For 9 of Block A:
CUTTING CHART

	Quantity	Length	Position
Ivory	18	6½"	#9, 10
	18	4½"	#7, 8
	18	1½"	#2, 6
	36	1½"	large "c" at bottom of heart
	36	1" x 1"	small "c" at top of heart
Red	18	4½"	#3, 4
	18	3½"	#1, 5

Block A – Heart Assembly:
   Refer to the Block A diagram. Note the position of the large and small "c" corners.
For each block:
   Align a small Ivory "c" square at the top of #1, 3, 4, & 5.
   Align a large Ivory "c" square at the bottom of #1, 3, 4, & 5.
   Refer to the Snowball Corner instructions.
   Sew on the diagonal, fold back the pieces and press.
   Sew #7 and #8 on the top and bottom of the piece. Press.
   Sew #9 and #10 to the left and right side of the piece. Press.
   Make 9 blocks.

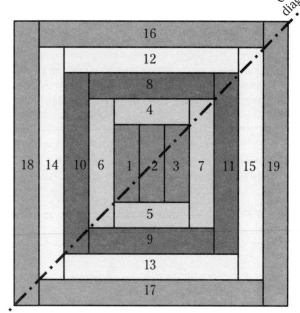

Table Runner End Block

TABLE RUNNER END ASSEMBLY:

Refer to the Table Runner End diagram.
Sew #1-2-3. Press.
Sew #4 and #5 to the top and bottom of the piece. Press.
Sew #6 and #7 to the left and right sides of the piece. Press.
Sew #8 and #9 to the top and bottom of the piece. Press.
Sew #10 and #11 to the left and right sides of the piece. Press.
Sew #12 and #13 to the top and bottom of the piece. Press.
Sew #14 and #15 to the left and right sides of the piece. Press.
Sew #16 and #17 to the top and bottom of the piece. Press.
Sew #18 and #19 to the left and right sides of the piece. Press.
Cut the piece on 1 diagonal.

For 1 of Table Runner End Block:

CUTTING CHART

	Quantity	Length	Position
Blue	3	3½"	#1, 2, 3
Green	2	3½"	#4, 5
	2	5½"	#6, 7
Red	2	5½"	#8, 9
	2	7½"	#10, 11
Ivory	2	7½"	#12, 13
	2	9½"	#14, 15
Aqua	2	9½"	#16, 17
	2	11½"	#18, 19

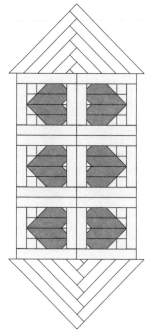

Sew ends to the runner.

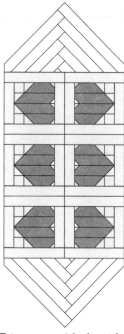

Trim even with the sides.

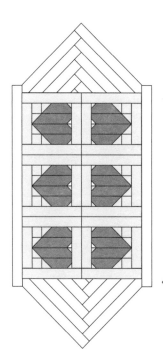

Sew side borders #1.

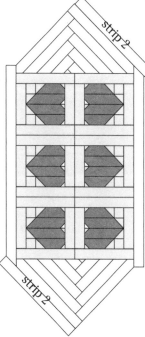

Sew end border strips #2.

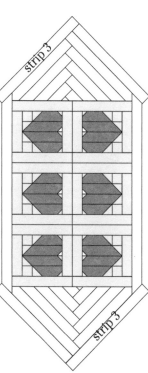

Sew end border strips #3.

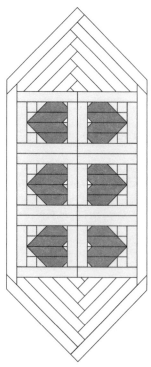

Trim ends even with sides.

Table Runner

Refer to the Table Runner Assembly diagram and note the position of the hearts.

Arrange all blocks on a work surface or table.

Sew 2 rows of 3 hearts each. Press.

Sew the rows together. Press.

Center, pin and sew an End piece on each end of the runner. Press.

Trim the edges even with the long side of the runner.

Borders: Cut 2 Green strips 20½". Label these #1.

Cut 2 Green strips 11½". Label these #2.

Cut 2 Green strips 12½". Label these #3.

Sew a Green border #1 to each long side of runner. Press. Trim as needed.

Sew a Green border #2 to one side of each "V" as shown in the diagram. Press. Trim as needed.

Sew a Green border #3 to the remaining side of each "V" as shown in the diagram. Press. Trim as needed.

Quilting: See Basic Instructions.

Binding: Cut strips 2½" wide.
Sew together end to end to equal 96".
See Binding Instructions.

Placemat

Sew 2 pieced heart blocks together. Press.

Cut 1 Brown and 1 Green strip 25½".

Sew the strips together. Press.

Cut the piece into 2 sections 2½" x 12½".

With the Brown on the outside, sew a strip to the top and bottom of the mat. Press.

Cut 2 Brown 10½" strips.

Sew a strip to the left and right sides of the mat. Press.

Quilting: See Basic Instructions.

Binding: Cut strips 2½" wide.
Sew together end to end to equal 58".
See Binding Instructions.

Hearts Placemat Assembly

Hearts Table Runner Assembly

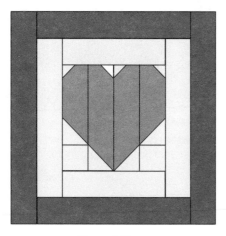

Pieced Heart
Potholder Assembly

Applique Heart
Potholder Assembly

Potholders

Pieced Heart Potholder:
Cut 2 Brown top/bottom borders 1½" x 6½".
Sew borders to the piece. Press.
Cut 2 Brown side borders 1½" x 8½".
Sew borders to the piece. Press.
Follow the instructions for Finishing Potholder.

Applique Heart Potholder:
Cut 6 Ivory strips 6½" long.
Sew the strips together. Press.
Cut 2 Blue side borders 1½" x 6½".
Sew borders to the piece. Press.
Cut 2 Blue top/bottom borders 1½" x 8½".
Sew borders to the piece. Press.
Cut 3 Red strips 4" long.
Sew the strips together to make a piece 3½" x 4". Press.
Use this piece to cut out the applique heart.
Refer to the Applique Instructions.
Applique as desired.
Follow the instructions for Finishing Potholder.

FINISHING POTHOLDER:
Quilting: See Basic Instructions.
Binding: For each potholder, cut a strip 2½" x 42".
See Binding Instructions.
Add a loop to the upper left corner if desired.

Heart Applique Potholder Pattern

March - Flowers

photo on page 6

SIZE: Table Runner: 17" x 35"
       Placemat: 13" x 19"
       Potholders: 7" x 7"

YARDAGE:

We used a *Moda* "Patisserie" by Fig Tree Quilts 'Honey Bun' collection of 1½" fabric strips - we purchased 1 'Honey Bun'

7 strips	OR	⅓ yard Cream
5 strips	OR	¼ yard Peach
4 strips	OR	⅙ yard Red
4 strips	OR	⅙ yard Pink
5 strips	OR	¼ yard Brown
3 strips	OR	⅛ yard Green
2 strips	OR	⅛ yard Tan

Binding   Purchase ½ yard
Backing   Purchase 1 yard
Batting   Purchase 36" x 37"
Sewing machine, needle, thread

FABRIC FOR INDIVIDUAL PROJECTS:

Fabric or Scraps for Table Runner:

5 strips	OR	7½" x 44" of Cream (¼ yard)
4 strips	OR	6" x 44" of Peach (⅙ yard)
3 strips	OR	4½" x 44" of Brown (⅛ yard)
3 strips	OR	4½" x 44" of Pink (⅛ yard)
3 strips	OR	4½" x 44" of Red (⅛ yard)
2 strips	OR	3" x 44" of Green
Binding		Purchase 2½" x 110" (¼ yard)
Backing		Purchase ⅝ yard
Batting		Purchase 19" x 37"

Fabric or Scraps for Placemat:

2 strips	OR	3" x 44" of Cream
2 strips	OR	3" x 44" of Brown
2 strips	OR	3" x 44" of Red
2 strips	OR	3" x 44" of Peach
1 strip	OR	1½" x 44" of Tan
1 strip	OR	1½" x 44" of Green
Binding		Purchase 2½" x 74" (⅙ yard)
Backing		Purchase 15" x 21"
Batting		Purchase 15" x 21"

Scraps for Each Potholder:

1 strip	OR	1½" x 44" of each color
Binding		Purchase 2½" x 44" (⅛ yard)
Backing		Purchase 9" x 9"
Batting		Purchase 9" x 9"

PREPARATION FOR STRIPS:

Cut all strips 1½" by the width of fabric (usually 42" - 44").

SEW BLOCKS:

Refer to the Cutting Chart and Assembly instructions for each block.
Label the pieces as you cut.

Placemat

Refer to the Placemat Assembly diagram.
    Use 2 Red flower and 2 Red tulip blocks.
    Cut 3 Cream 7½" sashing strips.
    Sew Block A - Sash - Block B - Sash - Block A - Sash - Block B - Sash. Press

Border #1:
    Cut 2 Peach strips 1½" x 15½" for top and bottom.
    Cut 2 Peach strips 1½" x 9½" for sides.
    Sew top and bottom borders to mat. Press.
    Sew side borders to the mat. Press.

Top and Bottom Border #2:
    Cut 1 Tan and 1 Brown strip 1½" x 35".
    Sew the strips together to make a piece 2½" x 35". Press.
    Cut the strip into 2 sections 2½" x 17½".
    Sew top and bottom borders to mat. Press.

Border #3:
    Cut 2 Brown strips 1½" x 13½" for sides.
    Sew side borders to the mat. Press.

Quilting: See Basic Instructions.
Binding: Cut strips 2½" wide.
    Sew together end to end to equal 74".
    See Binding Instructions.

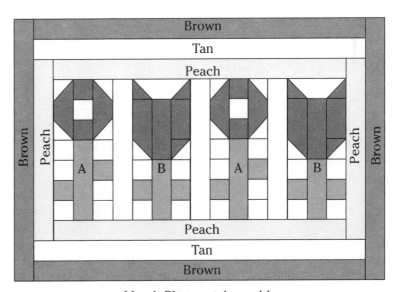

March Placemat Assembly

Block A - Flowers

For 7 with Red Flowers and 1 with Pink Flowers:

CUTTING CHART:

	Quantity	Length	Position
Cream	3	24"	Leaf section
	1	10½"	Flower center strip
	32	1½"	"c" corners
	1	1½"	Pink flower center
Red	14	3½"	Flower strips A & B
	2	10½"	Flower center strip
Pink	2	3½"	Flower strips A & B
	2	1½"	Flower center strip
Green	1	24"	Leaf section
	8	4½"	Stem

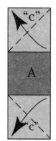

Folded Corners

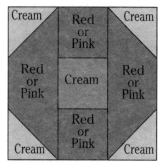

Flower Block
Make 7 Red and 1 Pink

24"

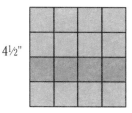

4½"

Leaf Sections:

Sew the 1½" x 24" strips
together side by side,
Cream - Cream - Green - Cream.
Press.
Cut into 16 leaf sections,
each 1½" x 4½".

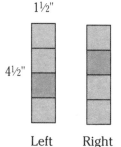

4½"

Cut 16 sections.
each 1½" x 4½".

1½"

Position Leaf Sections:

Left - Position 8 Leaf Sections
with the Green leaf
on the bottom.

Right - Position 8 Leaf Sections
with the Green leaf
on the top.

4½"

Left   Right

Stem Section:

Note the position of the
Green leaves on the '
each section.

Sew a Leaf Section to each
side of a Green
1½" x 4½" stem.
Press.
Make 8.

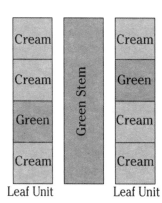

Leaf Unit   Leaf Unit
Stem Section - Make 8

Flower Block:

Make 7 Red and 1 Pink.

Corners:

Align a "c" Cream square on each end of a strip A.
Align a "c" Cream square on each end of a strip B.
Refer to the Snowball Corner instructions.
Sew on the diagonal, fold back the pieces and press.
Make 8 of side A and 8 of sides B.
For each A & B, 7 are Red and 1 is Pink = total 16.

Red Center strip:

Sew the 10½" strips together: Red - Cream - Red. Press.
Cut the piece into 7 sections, each 1½" x 3½".
Sew a strip "A" to the left side of a center. Press.
Sew a strip "B" to the right side of the center. Press.
Make 7.

Pink Center strip:

Sew the 1½" squares together: Pink - Cream - Pink. Press.
Sew a strip "A" to the left side of each center. Press.
Sew a strip "B" to the right side of each center. Press.
Sew a stem section to each flower section. Press.
Make 1.

Flowers: Sew finished Flower Sections to Leaf Sections. Press.

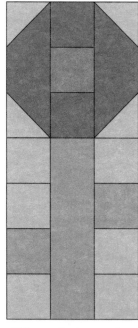

Finished Flower, Leaves and with Stem

Block B – Tulips

For 7 with Red Tulips and 1 with Pink Tulips:

CUTTING CHART:

	Quantity	Length	Position
Red	14	4½"	Tulip sides
	7	3½"	Tulip center
Pink	2	4½"	Tulip sides
	1	3½"	Tulip center
Green	1	24"	Leaf section
	8	3½"	Stem
Cream	2	24"	Leaf section
	32	1½"	"c" corners
	8	1½"	Top of Tulip center

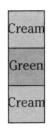

Cut 16 sections.
each 1½" x 3½".

Cut 8
Stems

Leaf Sections:

Sew the 24" strips together side by side,
Cream - Green - Cream. Press.
Cut into 16 pieces, each 1½" x 3½".

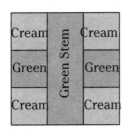

Leaf
Unit

Leaf
Unit

Stem Section - Make 8

Stem Section:

Sew a Leaf Section to each side of a Green
1½" x 3½" stem. Press.
Make 8.

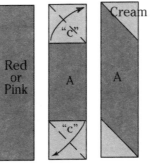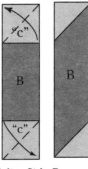

Tulip Side A
Folded Corners

Tulip Side B
Folded Corners

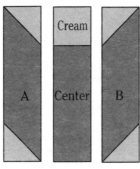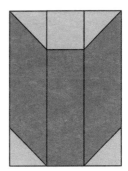

Tulip
Make 7 Red and 1 Pink

Tulip Finished

Tulip Block:

Make 7 Red and 1 Pink.

Corners:

Align a "c" Cream square on each end of strip "A".
Align a "c" Cream square on each end of strip "B".
Refer to the Snowball Corner instructions.
Sew on the diagonal, fold back the pieces and press.
Make 8 of side "A" and 8 of side "B".

Center strip:

Sew a Cream 1½" square to the top of each tulip center
(7 Red and 1 Pink).
Sew a side "A" to the left side of each center strip.
Sew a side "B" to the right side of each center strip. Press.

Tulips: Sew finished Tulip Sections to Leaf Sections. Press.

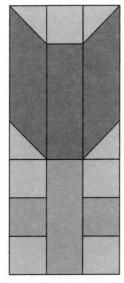

Finished Tulip, Leaves and with Stem

Table Runner

Refer to the Table Runner Assembly diagram.
Use 5 Red flower blocks and 5 Red tulip blocks.

Center: Cut 5 Pink 23½" strips.
Sew the strips together to make a piece 5½" x 23½".

Border #1:
Cut 2 Peach strips 1½" x 5½" for ends.
Cut 2 Peach strips 1½" x 25½" for sides.
Sew end borders to the table runner. Press.
Sew side borders to the table runner. Press.

Flower & Tulip Border #2:
Use the Red flower and tulip blocks to make this border.
Ends: Sew a Block A to one end and a Block B to the other end. Press.
Sashing: Cut 6 Peach 3½" sashing strips for side flower border.
Sides: Sew Block A - Sash - Block B - Sash - Block A - Sash - Block B. Press.
Sew to one side of the runner. Press.
Sew Block B - Sash - Block A - Sash - Block B - Sash - Block A. Press.
Sew to the remaining side of the runner. Press.

Border #3:
Cut 2 Peach strips 1½" x 13½" for ends.
Cut 2 Peach strips 1½" x 33½" for sides.
Sew end borders to the table runner. Press.
Sew side borders to the table runner. Press.

Border #4:
Cut 2 Brown strips 1½" x 15½" for ends.
Cut 2 Brown strips 1½" x 35½" for sides.
Sew end borders to the table runner. Press.
Sew side borders to the table runner. Press.

Quilting: See Basic Instructions.
Binding: Cut strips 2½" wide.
Sew together end to end to equal 110".
See Binding Instructions.

March Table Runner Assembly

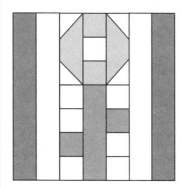

Flower Potholder
Assembly

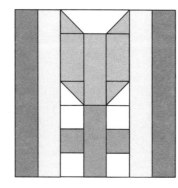

Tulip Potholder
Assembly

Potholders

Refer to the Potholder Assembly diagram.
Use 1 Pink flower block and 1 Pink tulip block.
Cut 2 Tan and 2 Brown strips 1½" x 15".
Sew 1 Tan and 1 Brown together to make a piece 2½" x 15". Press.
Cut the strip into 2 sections 2½" x 7½".
Repeat for the other 2 strips.
Sew a section to the right and left side of Blocks A and B. Press.
Quilting: See Basic Instructions.
Binding: Cut strips 2½" wide.
Sew together end to end to equal 76".
See Binding Instructions.
Add a loop to the upper left corner if desired.

April – Baskets

photo on page 7

SIZE:　Table Runner: 16" x 31"
　　　　Placemat: 13" x 18"
　　　　Potholders: 7" x 7"

YARDAGE:
We used a *Moda* "Sweet" by Urban Chiks
　'Honey Bun' collection of 1½" fabric strips
　- we purchased 1 'Honey Bun'

11 strips	OR	½ yard White prints
5 strips	OR	¼ yard Aqua
4 strips	OR	⅙ yard Green
4 strips	OR	⅙ yard Red
4 strips	OR	⅙ yard Pink
2 strips	OR	⅛ yard Orange

Binding　　　Purchase ⅞ yard
Backing　　　Purchase 1 yard
Batting　　　Purchase 36" x 36"
Sewing machine, needle, thread
DMC pearl cotton or 6-ply floss
#22 or #24 chenille needle

FABRIC FOR INDIVIDUAL PROJECTS:
Fabric or Scraps for Table Runner:
6 strips	OR	9" x 44" of White (¼ yard)
3 strips	OR	4½" x 44" of Green (⅛ yard)
3 strips	OR	4½" x 44" of Red (⅛ yard)
2 strips	OR	3" x 44" of Orange
2 strips	OR	3" x 44" of Aqua
2 strips	OR	3" x 44" of Pink
Applique		4½" x 16½" of Red or Pink for flowers
		1½" x 18½" of Green for leaves
		1½" x 3½" of Scraps for flower centers

Binding　Purchase 2½" x 132" (⅓ yard)
Backing　Purchase ½ yard
Batting　Purchase 18" x 33"

Fabric or Scraps for Placemat:
3 strips	OR	4½" x 44" of White (⅛ yard)
2 strips	OR	3" x 44" of Aqua
1 strip	OR	1½" x 44" of Red
1 strip	OR	1½" x 44" of Orange
1 strip	OR	1½" x 44" of Pink
1 strip	OR	1½" x 44" of Green
Applique		4½" x 4½" of Red, Pink, Green
		1½" x 5" of Green for leaves
		1½" x 3½" of Scraps for flower centers

Binding　Purchase 2½" x 72" of Aqua (⅙ yard)
Backing　Purchase 15" x 20"
Batting　Purchase 15" x 20"

Scraps for Each Potholder:
1 strip	OR	1½" x 44" of each color
Applique		4½" x 4½" of each color
Binding		Purchase 2½" x 44" (⅛ yard)
Backing		Purchase 9" x 9"
Batting		Purchase 9" x 9"

PREPARATION FOR STRIPS:
　Cut all strips 1½" by the width of fabric
　　(usually 42" - 44").
　Label the stacks or pieces as you cut.

SEW BLOCKS:
　Refer to the Cutting Chart and Assembly instructions
　　for each block.
　Label the pieces as you cut.

Snowball Corners
　Several strips in each block use the Snowball Corner technique. The direction of the diagonal for each strip in the block varies, so you must carefully note the diagonal on the block assembly diagram. Some strips have a corner on only one end. The squares used as Corners are labelled with a "c" in the cutting list.
　TIP: Fold back the triangle and check its position before you sew.
　STEPS: Align a square with the appropriate end of the strip and sew on the diagonal line. Fold the triangle back, press before attaching it to any other strips.

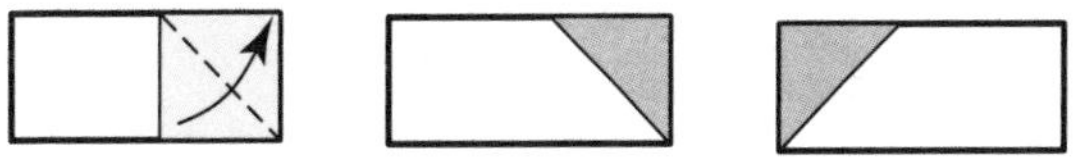

PREPARATION FOR APPLIQUE:
　Refer to the patterns on page 38.

For each Large Flower:
　Cut 3 strips 4".
　Sew the strips together to make a piece 3½" x 4".
　Cut a large Flower from each piece. Make 7.

For Small Pink Flowers:
　Cut 2 Pink 18½" strips.
　Sew the strips together to make a piece 2½" x 18½".
　Cut 6 small Flowers.

Large Flower Centers:
　Cut 7 circles 1½" in diameter.

Small Flower Centers:
　Cut 6 circles 1¼" in diameter.

Leaves:
　Cut 14 Green leaves (6 large and 8 small).

APPLIQUE: Refer to the Applique Instructions.
　Applique a large and small flower on each basket block.
　Set aside 1 large and 1 small flower for the potholder
　　with the flower pot.
　Applique as desired.
　Embroider the stems with a Running stitch.

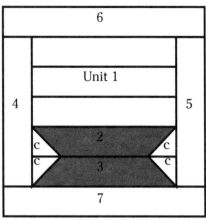

Block A

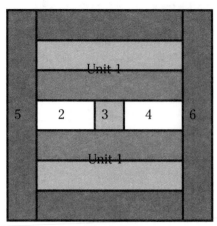

Block B

For 6 of Block A:
CUTTING CHART

	Quantity	Length	Position
Red	12	5½"	#2, 3
White	3	33"	Unit 1
	12	7½	#6, 7
	12	5½"	#4, 5
	24	1½"	"c" corners

5½"

3½"

Cut 6

BLOCK A ASSEMBLY:
Refer to the Block A diagram.

Unit 1:
Sew 3 White strips together to make a piece
   3½" x 33". Press.
Cut into 6 sections, each 3½" x 5½".

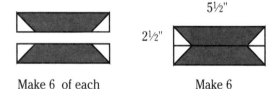

5½"

2½"

Make 6 of each   Make 6

Basket:
Label 6 Red strips #2 and 6 Red strips #3.
Align 1 White "c" square on both ends of
   each Red strip.
Carefully note the direction of the diagonal on
   strips #2 and #3.
Refer to the Snowball Corner instructions.
Sew on the diagonal, fold back the pieces and
   press. Make 12.
For each basket, sew #2 to #3. Press.

Assembly:
Sew a Unit 1 to a Basket section. Press.
Sew White #4 and #5 to the left and right sides
   of the piece. Press.
Sew White #6 and #7 to the top and bottom of
   the piece. Press. Make 6 blocks.

For 4 of Block B:
CUTTING CHART

	Quantity	Length	Position
Orange	1	44"	Unit 1
Pink	1	44"	Unit 1
Aqua	1	44"	Unit 1
	8	7½	#5, 6
White	8	2½"	#2, 4
Green	4	1½"	#3

5½"

3½"

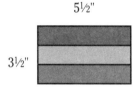

Cut 4

BLOCK B ASSEMBLY:
Refer to the Block B diagram.

Unit 1:
Sew three 44" strips together:
   Orange - Pink - Aqua to make a piece 3½" x 44".
   Press.
Cut into 8 sections, each 3½" x 5½".

5½"

1½"

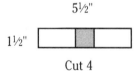

Cut 4

Center Row:
Sew a #2 - 3 - 4 to make a piece 1½" x 5½". Press.
   Make 4.

Assembly:
With Aqua on the outside of the block, arrange
   a Unit 1 - Center Row - Unit 1 on a work surface.
Sew the rows together. Press.
Sew #5 and #6 to the left and right sides of the block.
   Press. Make 4 blocks.

Table Runner

Refer to the Table Runner Assembly diagram.
Arrange all blocks on a work surface or table.

Rows 1 & 3:
Sew 2 of Block A together. Press.
Repeat for the other end (row 3).

Row 2:
Sew 2 of Block B together. Press.
Noting the orientation of the flower pots, sew
the rows together.

Side Borders:
Cut 2 Green strips 21½" long.
Sew a strip to the right and left sides of the
runner. Press.

End Sections:
Cut the following strips:
> 2 Orange 16½"
> 2 White 14½"
> 2 Aqua 12½"
> 2 White 10½"
> 2 Green 8½"

For each end, sew a set of strips together, O-W-A-W-G,
centering them to create 2 staggered edges.
Sew an End Section to each end of the table runner. Press.

Diagonal and End Borders:
Cut 4 Green strips 11" long.
Align each strip on an angle along the staggered edge of
each border.
Pin and sew each strip in place. Trim as needed. Press.

Quilting: See Basic Instructions.
Binding: Cut strips 2½" wide.
Sew together end to end to equal 106".
See Binding Instructions.

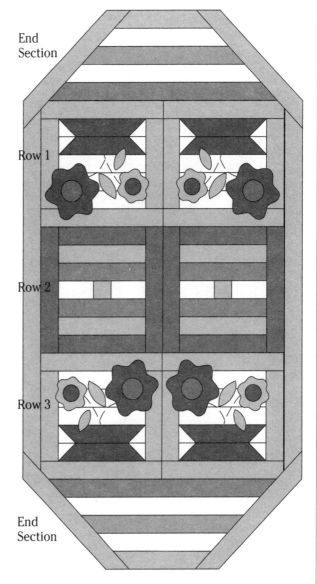

April Table Runner Assembly Diagram

Placemat

Sew a Block A to a Block B. Press.
Top & Bottom Borders:
Cut a Red, White and Aqua strip 29" long.
Sew the strips together Red - White - Aqua to
make a piece 3½" x 29".
Cut into 2 strips 3½" x 14½".
With the Aqua on the outside, sew a strip to the
top and bottom of the mat. Press.
Side Borders:
Cut a White and Aqua strip 27" long.
Sew the strips together to make a piece 2½" x 27".
Cut into 2 strips 2½" x 13½".
With the Aqua on the outside, sew a strip to the
right and left sides of the mat. Press.
Quilting: See Basic Instructions.
Binding: Cut strips 2½" wide.
Sew together end to end to equal 72".
See Binding Instructions.

April Placemat Assembly Diagram

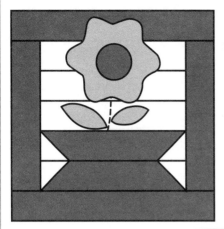

Block A

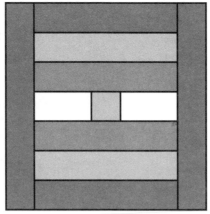

Block B

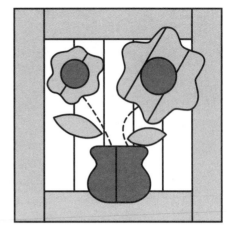

Flower Pot

Potholders

Use 1 of Block A and 1 of Block B to make potholders.

FINISHING THE POTHOLDERS:
Quilting: See Basic Instructions.
Binding: For each potholder, cut a strip 2½" x 38".
See Binding Instructions.

Sew a loop in the upper left corner if desired.

Flower Pot Applique Potholder:
Cut 5 White strips 5½" long.
Sew the strips together.

Top and Bottom Borders:
Cut 2 Pink 5½" strips.
Sew a strip to the top and bottom
of the piece. Press.

Side Borders:
Cut 2 Pink 7½" strips.
Sew a strip to the left and right sides
of the piece. Press.
Sew 2 Red 2½" scraps together to
make a piece for cutting out the
pitcher applique.
Applique pitcher, flowers and leaves.
Embroider a stem using a Running stitch.

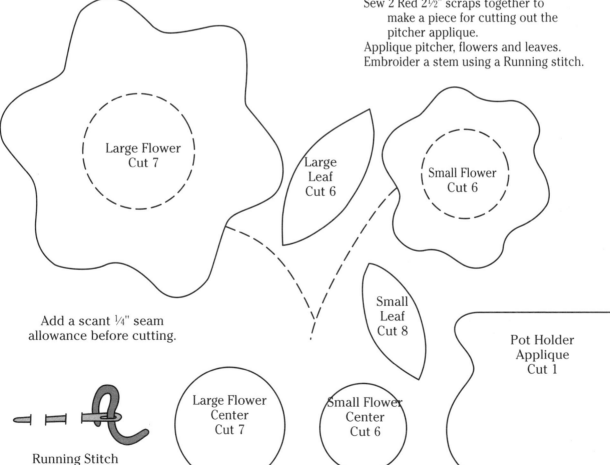

Large Flower
Cut 7

Large
Leaf
Cut 6

Small Flower
Cut 6

Small
Leaf
Cut 8

Add a scant ¼" seam
allowance before cutting.

Pot Holder
Applique
Cut 1

Running Stitch

Large Flower
Center
Cut 7

Small Flower
Center
Cut 6

May – Favorite Things

photo on page 8

SIZE: Table Runner: 16" x 30"
           Placemat: 11" x 16"
           Potholders: 7" x 7"

YARDAGE FOR PROJECTS:

We used a *Moda* "Hello Betty" by Chloe's Closet
    'Honey Bun' collection of 1½" fabric strips
    - we purchased 1 'Honey Bun'

7 strips	OR	⅓ yard White
5 strips	OR	¼ yard Blue
6 strips	OR	¼ yard Green
5 strips	OR	¼ yard Pink
4 strips	OR	⅙ yard Yellow
3 strips	OR	⅛ yard Red

Binding   Purchase 1 yard
Backing   Purchase 1 yard
Batting   Purchase 36" x 36"
Sewing machine, needle, thread
Buttons   7 Black ⁵⁄₁₆"; 6 Red 1"
DMC pearl cotton or 6-ply floss
#22 or #24 chenille needle

PREPARATION FOR STRIPS:
    Cut all strips 1½" by the width of fabric (usually 42" - 44").

SEW BLOCKS:
    Refer to the Cutting Chart and Assembly instructions
        for each block. Label the pieces as you cut.

FABRIC FOR INDIVIDUAL PROJECTS:

Fabric or Scraps for Table Runner:

4 strips	OR	6" x 44" of White (⅙ yard)
4 strips	OR	6" x 44" of Green (⅙ yard)
3 strips	OR	4½" x 44" of Blue (⅛ yard)
2 strips	OR	3" x 44" of Red
2 strips	OR	3" x 44" of Pink
2 strips	OR	3" x 44" of Yellow

Binding   Purchase 2½" x 102" (¼ yard)
Backing   Purchase ½ yard
Batting   Purchase 18" x 32"
Buttons   Purchase 4 Black ⁵⁄₁₆"; 3 Red 1"
DMC pearl cotton or 6-ply floss
#22 or #24 chenille needle

Snowball Corners

    Several strips in each block use the Snowball Corner technique. The direction of the diagonal for each strip in the block varies, so you must carefully note the diagonal on the block assembly diagram. Some strips have a corner on only one end. The squares used as Corners are labelled with a "c" in the cutting list.

    TIP: Fold back the triangle and check its position before you sew.

    STEPS: Align a square with the appropriate end of the strip and sew on the diagonal line. Fold the triangle back, press before attaching it to any other strips.

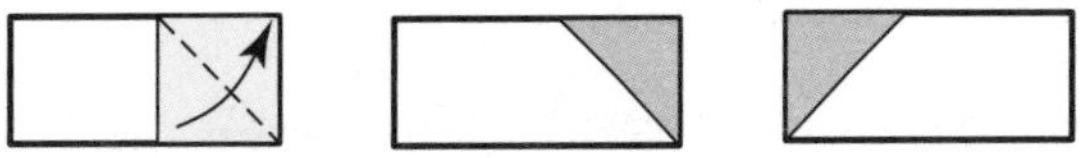

Fabric or Scraps for Placemat:

3 strips	OR	4½" x 44" of Pink (⅛ yard)
1 strip	OR	1½" x 44" of Red
1 strip	OR	1½" x 44" of Blue
1 strip	OR	1½" x 44" of White
1 strip	OR	1½" x 44" of Yellow
1 strip	OR	1½" x 44" of Green

Binding   Purchase 2½" x 64" (⅙ yard)
Backing   Purchase 13" x 18"
Batting   Purchase 13" x 18"
Buttons   Purchase 3 Red 1"
DMC pearl cotton or 6-ply floss
#22 or #24 chenille needle

Scraps for Each Potholder:

1 strip	OR	1½" x 44" of each color

Binding   Purchase 2½" x 44" (⅛ yard)
Backing   Purchase 9" x 9"
Batting   Purchase 9" x 9"
Buttons   Purchase 3 Black ⁵⁄₁₆"
DMC pearl cotton or 6-ply floss
#22 or #24 chenille needle

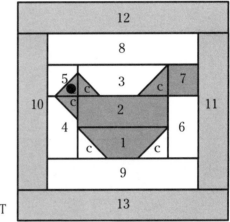

For 1 of Bird – Block A

CUTTING CHART

	Quantity	Length	Position
Blue	2	3½"	#1, 2
	2	1½"	#3c, 7
	3	1" x 1"	#3c, 4c, 5c
White	2	7½	#8, 9
	1	3½"	#3
	2	2½"	#4, 6
	3	1½"	#1c, 1c, 5
Pink	2	7½	#12, 13
	2	5½"	#10, 11

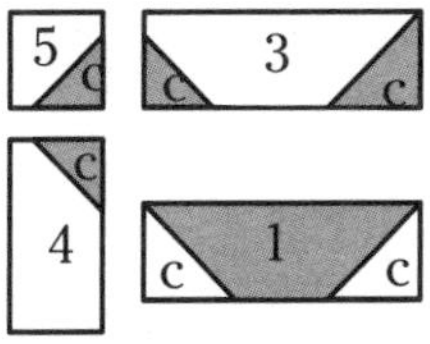

ASSEMBLY:
    Align 1 small Blue "c" square on #5.
    Align 1 small "c" square on #4.
    Align 2 large Blue "c" squares on #1.
    Align 2 Blue "c" squares on #3 (the 1½" square #3c is
        on the right end of #3).
    Refer to Snowball Corner instructions.
    Sew on the diagonal, fold back the pieces and press.
    Sew 1-2-3. Press.
    Sew 4-5. Press.
    Sew 6-7. Press.
    Sew 4-5 to the left of 1-2-3. Press.
    Sew 6-7 to the right of 1-2-3. Press.
    Sew 8 and 9 to the top and bottom of piece. Press.
    Sew 10 and 11 to the right and left sides of piece. Press.
    Sew 12 and 13 to the top and bottom of the piece. Press.

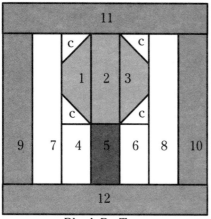

Block B - Tree

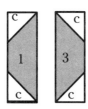

For 2 of Tree – Block B

CUTTING CHART

	Quantity	Length	Position
Green	6	3½"	#1, 2, 3
White	4	5½"	#7, 8
	4	2½"	#4, 6
	8	1½"	#1c, 1c, 3c, 3c
Red	2	2½"	#5
Blue	4	7½"	#11, 12
	4	5½"	#9, 10

ASSEMBLY:

Align 2 White "c" squares on #1.
Align 2 White "c" squares on #3.
Refer to the Snowball Corner instructions.
Sew on the diagonals, fold back the pieces and press.
Sew 1-2-3. Press.
Sew 4-5-6. Press.
Sew 1-2-3 to 4-5-6. Press.
Sew #7 and 8 to the left and right sides of the piece.
  Press.
Sew 9 and 10 to the right and left sides of piece. Press.
Sew 11 and 12 to the top and bottom of the piece.
  Press.

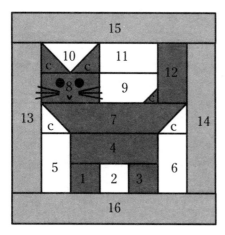

Block C - Cat

Cat Whiskers Pattern

For 2 of Cat – Block C

CUTTING CHART

	Quantity	Length	Position
White	10	2½"	#5, 6, 9, 10, 11
	6	1½"	#2, 7c, 7c
Red	2	5½"	#7
	2	3½"	#4
	4	2½"	#8, 12
	8	1½"	#1, 3, 10c, 10c
	2	1" x 1"	#9c
Green	4	7½"	#15, 16
	4	5½"	#13, 14

ASSEMBLY:

Align 2 White "c" squares on #7.
Align 2 Red "c" squares on #10.
Align 1 small Red "c" square on #9.
Refer to the Snowball Corner instructions.
Sew on the diagonal, fold back pieces and press.
Sew 1-2-3. Press.
Sew #4 to the top of 1-2-3. Press.
Sew 5 and 6 to the left and right sides of unit. Press.
Sew #7 to the top of the piece. Press.
Sew 8-9. Press.
Sew 10-11. Press.
Sew 8-9 to 10-11. Press.
Sew 12 to the right side of the 8-9-10-11. Press.
Sew 8-9-10-11-12 to the top of the piece. Press.
Sew 13 and 14 to the right and left sides of piece. Press.
Sew 15 and 16 to the top and bottom of the piece.
  Press.
When the project is finished, sew 2 buttons for the eyes
  and embroider the mouth and whiskers.

For 2 of House – Block D

CUTTING CHART

	Quantity	Length	Position
White	12	1½"	#8c, 8c, 9c, 9c, 10, 11
Blue	2	5½"	#8
	2	3½"	#9
	2	2½"	#5
	2	1½"	#1
Red	2	5½"	#7
	6	2½"	#3, 4, 6
	2	1½"	#2
Yellow	4	5½"	#12, 13
	4	7½"	#14, 15

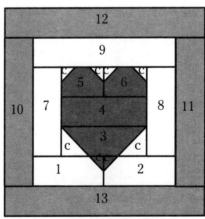

Block D - House

ASSEMBLY:

Align 2 White "c" squares on #8.
Align 2 White "c" squares on #9.
Refer to Snowball Corner instructions.
Sew on the diagonal, fold back pieces and press.
Sew 1-2. Press.
Sew #3 to the left side of 1-2. Press.
Sew 4-5-6. Press.
Sew 4-5-6 to the right side of 1-2-3. Press.
Sew 9-10-11. Press. Sew 7-8-9. Press.
Sew 7-8-9 to the top of the piece. Press.
Sew 12 and 13 to the left and right sides of the piece. Press.
Sew 14 and 15 to the top and bottom of the piece. Press.

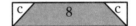

For 2 of Small Heart – Block E

CUTTING CHART

	Quantity	Length	Position
White	2	5½"	#9
	4	3½"	#7, 8
	4	3"	#1, 2
	4	1½"	#3c, 3c
	8	1"x 1"	#5c, 5c, 6c, 6c
Red	4	3½"	#3, 4
	4	2"	#5, 6
	4	1"x 1"	#1c, 2c
Blue	4	7½"	#12, 13
	4	5½"	#10, 11

Block E - Small Heart

ASSEMBLY:

Align 1 small White "c" square on #1.
Align 1 small White "c" square on #2.
Align 2 large White "c" squares on #3.
Align 2 small White "c" squares on #5.
Align 2 small White "c" squares on #6.
Refer to Snowball Corner instructions.
Sew on the diagonal, fold back pieces, press.
Sew 1-2. Press.
Sew 5-6. Press.
Sew 3-4-5/6. Press.
Sew strips #7 and #8 to the left and right sides of the piece. Press.
Sew strip #9 to the top of the piece. Press.
Sew 1-2 to the bottom of the piece. Press.
Sew strips #10 and #11 to the left and right sides of the piece. Press.
Sew strips #12 and #13 to the top and bottom of piece. Press.

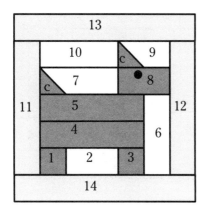

Block H - Scotty Dog

For 2 of Scotty Dog – Block H

CUTTING CHART

Quantity		Length	Position
Blue	4	4½"	#4, 5
	2	2½"	#8
	8	2½"	#1, 3, 7c, 9c
White	6	3½"	#6, 7, 10
	4	2½"	#2, 9
Yellow	4	7½"	#13, 14
	4	5½"	#11, 12

ASSEMBLY:

Align 1 Blue "c" square on #7.
Align 1 Blue "c" square on #9.
Refer to the Snowball Corner instructions.
Sew on the diagonal, fold back the pieces and press.
Sew 1-2-3. Press.
Sew 4-5. Press.
Sew 4-5 to the top of 1-2-3. Press.
Sew #6 to the right side of the piece. Press.
Sew 7-8. Press.
Sew 9-10. Press.
Sew 7-8 and 9-10 to the top of the piece. Press.
Sew #11 and #12 to the left and right sides of the piece. Press.
Sew #13 and #14 to the top and bottom of the piece. Press.
When the project is finished, sew on a button for the eye.

Block F - Butterfly

For 2 of Butterfly – Block F

CUTTING CHART

Quantity		Length	Position
White	14	1½"	#5, "c"
Pink	4	5½"	#3, 6
	4	4½"	#2, 7
	4	1¾"	#1, 8
Blue	2	4½"	#4
Green	4	7½"	#11, 12
	4	5½"	#9, 10

Butterfly
Antenna
Embroidery
Pattern

ASSEMBLY:

Align 1 White "c" square on #2
Align 1 White "c" square on #7.
Align 1 White "c" square on #3.
Align 1 White "c" square on #6.
NOTE: Aligning a "c" square on the end of #1 and #8 may seem a little tricky. Simply align it along the edge, notice the direction of the diagonal, and sew it in place. (Do not sew two 1½"x 1½" squares to make half square triangles or they will turn out too small.)
Align 1 White "c" square on #1.
Align 1 White "c" square on #8.
Refer to Snowball Corner instructions.
Sew on the diagonal, fold back pieces and press.
Sew 1-2. Press.
Sew 4-5. Press.
Sew 7-8. Press.
Sew the columns together. Press.
Sew #9 and #10 to the left and right sides of the piece. Press.
Sew #11 and #12 to the top and bottom of the piece. Press.

NOTE: Since the antennae extend beyond the block. Do the embroidery after blocks are assembled.

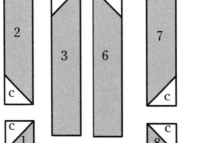

Running Stitch

For 2 of Flower Pot – Block G

CUTTING CHART

	Quantity	Length	Position
White	4	5½"	#6, 7
	6	3½"	#1, 2, 3
Blue	4	3½"	#4, 5
Red	2	8"	Applique flowers
Green	2	7½"	Applique leaves
Pink	4	7½"	#10, 11
	4	5½"	#8, 9

ASSEMBLY:

Sew 1-2-3. Press.
Sew 4-5. Press.
Sew 1-2-3 to 4-5. Press.
Sew #6 and #7 to the left and
    right sides of the piece. Press.
Sew #8 and #9 to the left and
    right sides of the piece. Press.
Sew #10 and #11 to the top and
    bottom of the piece. Press.
Refer to the Finishing section
    for Applique instructions.
Applique the flowers and leaves at
    this time if desired.

When the project is finished, sew
    on buttons for flower centers.

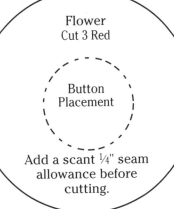

Leaf
Cut 3 Green
Add a scant ¼" seam
allowance before
cutting.

Flower
Cut 3 Red

Button
Placement

Add a scant ¼" seam
allowance before
cutting.

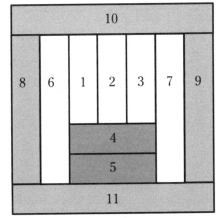

Block G - Flower Pot

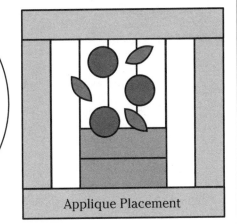

Applique Placement

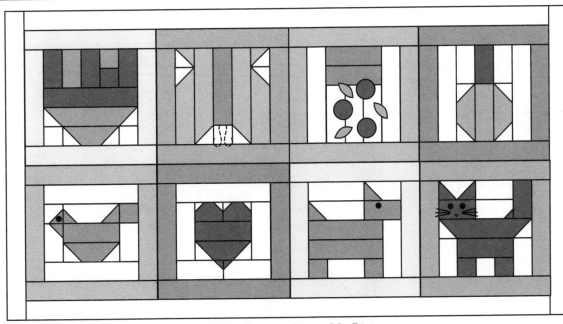

May Table Runner Assembly Diagram

Table Runner

Refer to the Table Runner Assembly diagram.
Arrange all blocks on a work surface or table.
Sew 2 rows of 4 blocks each. Press.
Sew the rows together. Press.

Border: Cut 2 Green strips 1½" x 28½" for top and bottom.
Cut 2 Green strips 1½" x 16½" for sides.
Sew top and bottom borders to the runner. Press.
Sew side borders to the runner. Press.

Quilting: See Basic Instructions.

Binding: Cut strips 2½" wide. Sew together end to end to equal 102".
See Binding Instructions.

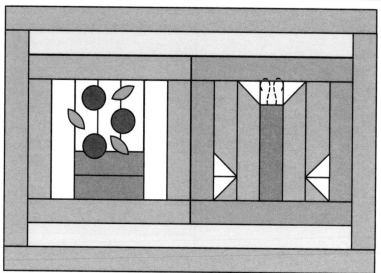

May Placemat Assembly

Placemat

Sew a Butterfly Block F to Basket Block G. Press.
Cut 2 Yellow strips 1½" x 14½".
Sew a strip to the top and bottom of the piece. Press.
Cut 2 Pink strips 1½" x 9½".
Sew a strip to the left and right sides of the piece. Press.
Cut 2 Pink strips 1½" x 16½".
Sew a strip to the top and bottom of the piece. Press.
Quilting: See Basic Instructions.
Binding: Cut strips 2½" wide.
Sew together end to end to equal 64".
See Binding Instructions.

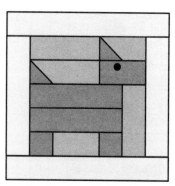

Scotty Dog Potholder

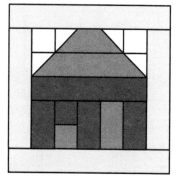

House Potholder

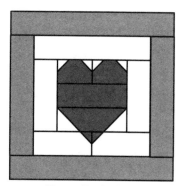

Heart Potholder

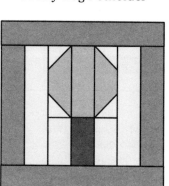

Tree Potholder

Cat Potholder

Potholders

Choose 6 blocks for Potholders.

Quilting: See Basic Instructions.

Binding: For each potholder, cut a
strip 2½" x 38".
See Binding Instructions.
Sew a loop in the upper left
corner if desired.

June - Flower Garden

Photo on page 9

SIZE: Table Runner: 16" x 41"
Placemat: 16" x 19"
Potholders: 7" x 7"

YARDAGE FOR PROJECTS:
We used a *Moda* "Soiree" by Lila Tueller
'Honey Bun' collection of 1½" fabric strips
- we purchased 1 'Honey Bun'

12 strips	OR	½ yard White
7 strips	OR	⅓ yard Green
5 strips	OR	¼ yard Golden
5 strips	OR	¼ yard Turquoise
3 strips	OR	⅛ yard Light Pink
3 strips	OR	⅛ yard Medium Pink

Binding   Purchase ⅝ yard
Backing   Purchase 1 yard
Batting   Purchase 36" x 44"
Sewing machine, needle, thread
DMC pearl cotton or 6-ply floss
#22 or #24 chenille needle

FABRIC FOR INDIVIDUAL PROJECTS:
Fabric or Scraps for Table Runner:

7 strips	OR	10½" x 44" of White (⅓ yard)
3 strips	OR	4½" x 44" of Green (⅛ yard)
4 strips	OR	6" x 44" of Golden (⅙ yard)
3 strips	OR	4½" x 44" of Turquoise (⅛ yard)
3 strips	OR	4½" x 44" of Light Pink (⅛ yard)
1 strip	OR	1½" x 44" of Med. Pink
Binding		Purchase 2½" x 110" (¼ yard)
Backing		Purchase ½ yard
Batting		Purchase 18" x 43"
Applique		Fabric included in strips

Fabric or Scraps for Placemat:

5 strips	OR	7½" x 44" of White (¼ yard)
3 strips	OR	4½" x 44" of Green (⅛ yard)
2 strips	OR	3" x 44" of Med. Pink
2 strips	OR	3" x 44" of Turquoise
Binding		Purchase 2½" x 70" (⅙ yard)
Backing		Purchase 18" x 21"
Batting		Purchase 18" x 21"
Applique		Fabric included in strips

Scraps for Each Potholder:

1 strip	OR	1½" x 44" of each color
Binding		Purchase 2½" x 44" (⅛ yard)
Backing		Purchase 9" x 9"
Batting		Purchase 9" x 9"
Applique		4½" x 4½" of Pink, Golden, Green

PREPARATION FOR STRIPS:
Cut all strips 1½" by the width of fabric
(usually 42" - 44").

SEW BLOCKS:
Refer to the Cutting Chart and Assembly instructions
for each block.
Label the pieces as you cut.

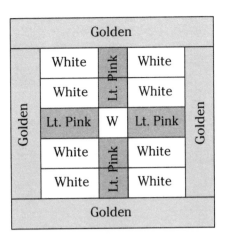

Block A

For 7 of Block A:
CUTTING CHART

	Quantity	Length	Position
White	4	35"	Unit 1
	1	10½"	Unit 2
Light Pink	1	35"	Unit 1
	4	10½"	Unit 2
Golden	14	7½"	Top & Bottom borders
	14	5½"	Side borders

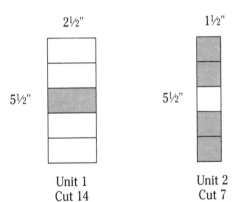

Unit 1
Cut 14

Unit 2
Cut 7

BLOCK A ASSEMBLY:
6 Blocks will be used in the Table Runner.
1 Block will be used for a Potholder.

Unit 1:
Sew the 35" strips together W - W - P - W - W to make a
piece 5½" x 35". Press.
Cut the piece into 14 sections 2½" x 5½".
Label each section Unit 1.

Unit 2:
Sew the 10½" strips together P - P - W - P - P to make a
piece 5½" x 10½". Press.
Cut the piece into 7 sections 1½" x 5½".
Label each section Unit 2.

Block Center: For each block, sew Unit 1 - Unit 2 - Unit 1. Press.

Borders:
Sew a 5½" Golden strip to the left and right sides of the
piece. Press.
Sew a 7½" Golden strip to the top and bottom. Press.

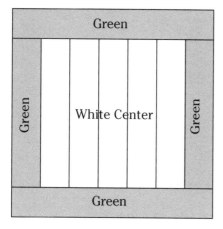

Block B

For 3 of Block B:

CUTTING CHART

	Quantity	Length	Position
White	5	16½"	Unit 3
Green	2	16½"	Unit 3
	6	7½"	Top & Bottom borders

BLOCK B ASSEMBLY:

2 Blocks will be used in the Placemat. 1 Block will be used for a Potholder.

Unit 3:

Sew the 16½" strips together Green - 5 White - Green
to make a piece 7½" x 16½". Press.
Cut the piece into 3 sections 5½" x 7½". Label each section Unit 3.

Borders:

Sew a 7½" Green strip to the top and bottom of the piece. Press.

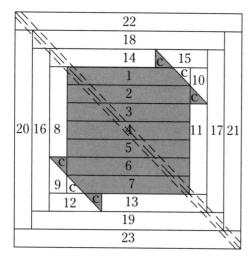

Block C - Make 2

For 2 of Basket Block C:

CUTTING CHART

	Quantity	Length	Position
White	4	13½"	#22, 23
	8	11½"	#18, 19, 20, 21
	4	9½"	#16, 17
	4	6½"	#13, 14
	4	5½"	#8, 11
	4	3½"	#12, 15
	4	2½"	#9, 10
	4	1½"	#1c, 7c
Turquoise	14	7½"	#1, 2, 3, 4, 5, 6, 7
	8	1½"	#9c, 10c, 12c, 15c

2½"

3½"

12

15

7½"

1

7

BLOCK C ASSEMBLY:

Make 2 blocks.
Cut each block on one diagonal as shown to yield 4 pieces.
Two pieces will be used in the Table Runner.
One piece will be used for a Placemat.
You will have 1 piece leftover.

Snowball Corners:

Refer to the Snowball Corners Instructions.
Align a Turquoise 1½" "c" square on the end of each #9, 10, 12, & 15.
Draw a diagonal line. Sew on the line. Fold the corner back. Press.
Cut off excess fabric from underneath.
Repeat with a White 1½" "c" square on each #1 and 7.

Refer to the Block C Assembly Diagram.

Sew 1-2-3-4-5-6-7 to form the center. Press.
Sew 8-9. Press. Sew 10-11. Press. Sew 12-13. Press. Sew 14-15. Press.
Sew 8-9 to the left side of the center. Press.
Sew 10-11 to the right side of the center. Press.
Sew 12-13 to the bottom of the piece. Press.
Sew 14-15 to the top of the piece. Press.
Sew #16 & #17 to the left and right sides of the piece. Press.
Sew #18 & #19 to the top and bottom of the piece. Press.
Sew #20 & #21 to the left and right sides of the piece. Press.
Sew #22 & #23 to the top and bottom of the piece. Press.

Make 2 Blocks. Cut each block on 1 diagonal as shown.

Snowball Corners

Several strips in each block use the Snowball Corner technique. The direction of the diagonal for each strip in the block varies, so you must carefully note the diagonal on the block assembly diagram. Some strips have a corner on only one end. The squares used as Corners are labelled with a "c" in the cutting list.

TIP: Fold back the triangle and check its position before you sew.

STEPS: Align a square with the appropriate end of the strip and sew on the diagonal line. Fold the triangle back, press before attaching it to any other strips.

Potholder

Block A - Potholder:
Follow the Finishing Potholder instructions.

Block B - Flower Applique Potholder:
For Flower Potholder, use 1 Block B.
Cut 4 Med Pink 4½" strips.
Sew strips together to make a piece 4½" x 4½".
Use this piece to cut out the flower.
Cut out a Green leaf and Golden center.
Refer to the Applique instructions.

FINISHING THE POTHOLDER
Quilting: See Basic Instructions.
Binding:
For each potholder, cut 1 Golden strip 2½" x 38".
See Binding Instructions.

Sew a loop to the upper left corner if desired.

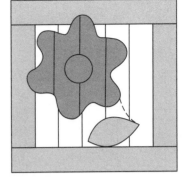

Block A
Potholder Diagram

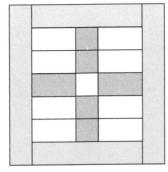

Flower Applique Diagram

Table Runner

Refer to the Table Runner Assembly diagram.
Arrange all blocks on a work surface or table.
Sew 3 rows of 2 Blocks A. Press.
Sew the rows together. Press.
Center and sew a Basket Block C to each end. Press.
Trim the edges even with the sides of the runner.

Border:
Cut 2 Green strips 1½" x 24½" for sides.
Cut 4 Green strips 1½" x 12½" for the ends.
Sew side borders to the runner. Press. Trim as needed.
Sew end borders to each side of the "V". Press.
Trim as needed.

Applique:

To make 4 Large Flowers:
Cut 4 Med Pink and 4 Turquoise 9" strips.
For each color, sew 4 strips together to make a piece 4½" x 9". Press.
Cut out 2 Med Pink and 2 Turquoise large flowers.

To make 2 Small Pink Flowers:
Cut 3 Pink 8" strips.
Sew the strips together to make a piece 3½" x 8". Press.
Cut out 2 small flowers.

Centers: Cut 4 Turquoise and 2 Med Pink 1½" circles.
Leaves: Cut 10 Green leaves.
Applique:
Refer to the Applique instructions. Applique as desired.
Embroider the stems with a Running stitch.

Optional - Outline Technique for Applique:
Using FabriTac or a clear washable glue, adhere Green pearl cotton around each applique shape.
Using a small width Zig-zag stitch, sew over the pearl cotton.

Quilting: See Basic Instructions.
Binding: Cut strips 2½" wide.
Sew together end to end to equal 110".
See Binding Instructions.

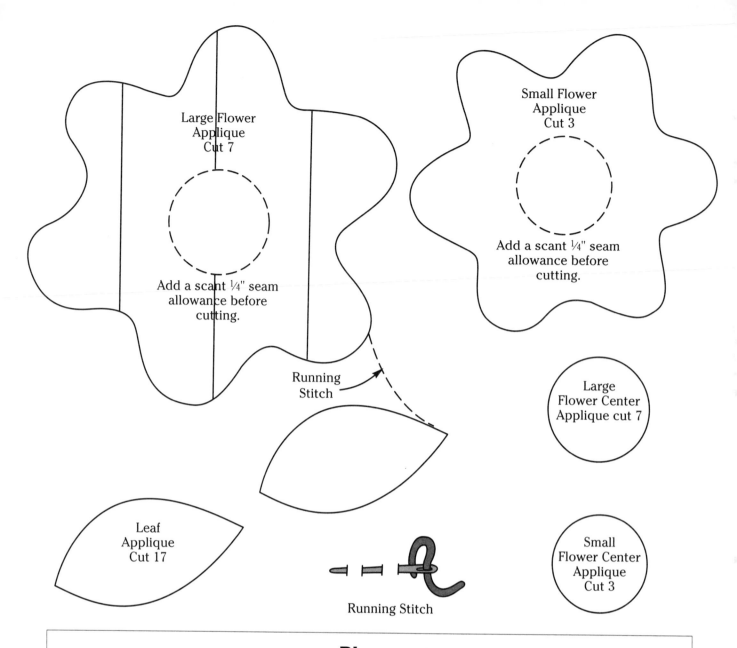

Large Flower
Applique
Cut 7

Add a scant ¼" seam
allowance before
cutting.

Small Flower
Applique
Cut 3

Add a scant ¼" seam
allowance before
cutting.

Running
Stitch

Large
Flower Center
Applique cut 7

Leaf
Applique
Cut 17

Small
Flower Center
Applique
Cut 3

Running Stitch

June Placemat Assembly

Placemat

Sew 2 of Block B together. Press.
Sew a Basket Block C to the bottom of
    the piece. Press.
Side Borders: Cut 2 Green 9½" strips.
    Sew a strip to the left and right sides of the mat. Press.
Top Border:
    Cut 1 Light Pink strip 16½".
    Sew the strip to the top of the mat. Press.
    Trim as needed.
Bottom Borders:
    Cut 2 Light Pink strips 12½".
    Sew a strip to each side of the point. Press.
Applique: Cut 4 Med Pink 9" strips.
    Cut 3 Turquoise 4" strips.
    Cut 3 1½" circles for flower centers and 4 leaves.
    Make 1 Small and 2 Large Flowers following the
      Applique instructions on page 45.
Quilting: See Basic Instructions.
Binding: Cut strips 2½" wide.
    Sew together end to end to equal 70".
    See Binding Instructions.

July - Picnic

hoto on page 10

ZE: Table Runner: 18" x 44"
Placemat: 13" x 20"
Potholders: 7" x 7"

ARDAGE:
'e used a *Moda* "Oh Cherry Oh" by Me & My Sister
'Honey Bun' collection of 1½" fabric strips
- we purchased 1 'Honey Bun'

12 strips	OR	½ yard White
5 strips	OR	¼ yard Lime Green
5 strips	OR	¼ yard Aqua
5 strips	OR	¼ yard Red
3 strips	OR	⅛ yard Pink
3 strips	OR	⅛ yard Yellow
nding	Purchase ⅝ yard	
acking	Purchase 1 yard	
atting	Purchase 36" x 46"	

ewing machine, needle, thread

ABRIC FOR INDIVIDUAL PROJECTS:

abric or Scraps for Table Runner:

8 strips	OR	12" x 44" of White (⅓ yard)
4 strips	OR	6" x 44" of Green (⅙ yard)
3 strips	OR	4½" x 44" of Red (⅛ yard)
3 strips	OR	4½" x 44" of Yellow (⅛ yard)
3 strips	OR	4½" x 44" of Aqua (⅛ yard)
2 strips	OR	3" x 44" of Pink
Binding	Purchase 2½" x 134" (⅓ yard)	
Backing	Purchase ⅝ yard	
Batting	Purchase 20" x 46"	
Applique		included in strips

abric or Scraps for Placemat:

3 strips	OR	4½" x 44" of White (⅛ yard)
2 strips	OR	3" x 44" of Red
2 strips	OR	3" x 44" of Aqua
1 strip	OR	1½" x 44" of Green
1 strip	OR	1½" x 44" of Pink
Binding	Purchase 2½" x 76" (⅙ yard)	
Backing	Purchase 15" x 22"	
Batting	Purchase 15" x 22"	
Applique	Purchase 1" Yellow; Aqua included in strips	

craps for Each Potholder:

1 strip	OR	1½" x 44" of each color
Binding	Purchase 2½" x 44" (⅛ yard)	
Backing	Purchase 9" x 9"	
Batting	Purchase 9" x 9"	
Applique		4½" x 6½" of Aqua, 1" Yellow

REPARATION FOR STRIPS:
Cut all strips 1½" by the width of fabric (usually 42" - 44").

EW BLOCKS:
Refer to the Cutting Chart and Assembly instructions for each block. Label the pieces as you cut.

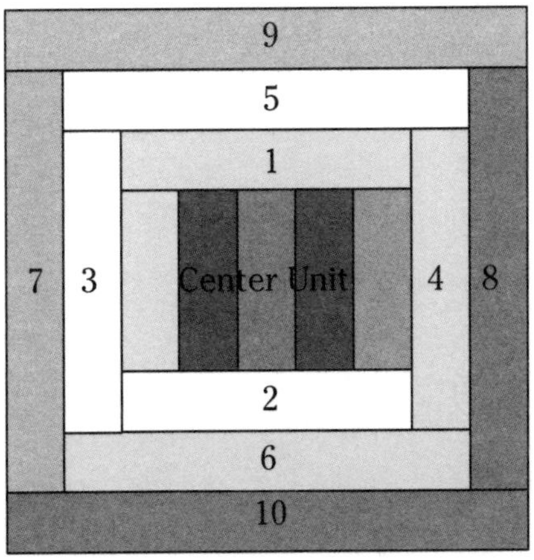

Block B for Table Runner

For 4 of Block B:

CUTTING CHART

Quantity		Length	Position
Yellow	1	14"	Center Unit
	8	5½"	#1, 4
	4	7½"	#6
Red	2	14"	Center Unit
Aqua	1	14"	Center Unit
	4	5½"	#2
Pink	1	14"	Center Unit
	4	7½"	#8
	4	9½"	#10
White	4	5½"	#3
	4	7½"	#5
Green	4	7½"	#7
	4	9½"	#9

5½"

3½"

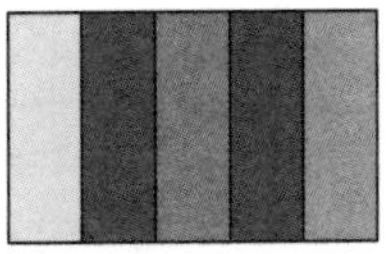

Cut 4

BLOCK B ASSEMBLY:

Center: Sew the 14" Center strips together: Y-R-P-R-A to make a piece 5½" x 14". Press.

Cut the strip into 4 pieces, each 3½" x 5½".
Refer to the Block B diagram.

Sew #1 and #2 to the top and bottom of the Center. Press.
Sew #3 and #4 to the left and right sides of the piece. Press.
Sew #5 and #6 to the top and bottom of the piece. Press.
Sew #7 and #8 to the left and right sides of the piece. Press.
Sew #9 and #10 to the top and bottom of the piece. Press.
Make 4 blocks.

Snowball Corners

Several strips in each block use the Snowball Corner technique. The direction of the diagonal for each strip in the block varies, so you must carefully note the diagonal on the block assembly diagram. Some strips have a corner on only one end. The squares used as Snowball Corners are labelled with a "c" in the cutting list.

TIP: Fold back the triangle and check its position before you sew.

STEPS: Align a square with the appropriate end of the strip and sew on the diagonal line. Fold the triangle back and press before attaching it to any other strips

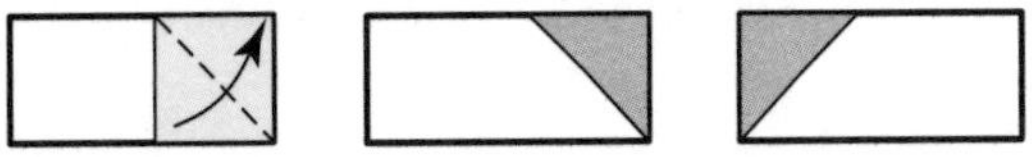

For 3 Watermelon Blocks:

CUTTING CHART

	Quantity	Length	Position
White	1	18"	Unit 1
	12	16½"	#5, 11, 12, 13
	6	9½"	Side Borders
	6	4½"	#4
	6	3½"	#3
	6	2½"	#2
Red	6	12½"	#6, 7
	3	10½"	#8
	3	8½"	#9
Green	1	18"	Unit 1
	3	8½"	#10
	12	1½"	#14, 15, 16, 17
	36	1½"	"c" corners

2½"

1½"

Unit 1
Make 12

Unit 1 Assembly:
Sew a White 18" strip and a Green 18"strip together side by side to make a piece 2½" x 18".
Cut the piece into 12 units, each 1½" x 2½".
Label the pieces Unit 1.

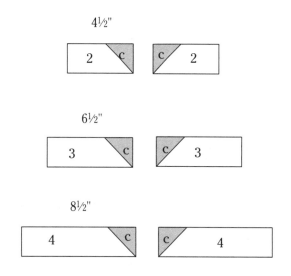

4½"

| 2 | c | | c | 2 |

6½"

| 3 | c | | c | 3 |

8½"

| 4 | c | | c | 4 |

Sew Snowball Corners to the White Strips:
Line up a Green "c" on one end of White #2.
Draw a diagonal line. Sew on the line.
Fold the corner back and press.
Cut off excess fabric from underneath.
Repeat with the second Green "c" and #2, being sure the diagonal is in the opposite direction.

Repeat with Green "c" on each White #3 & 4.

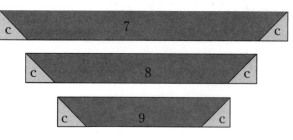

Sew Corners to the Red Strips:
Line up a Green "c" on one end of Red #7.
Draw a diagonal line. Sew on the line. Fold corner back. Press.
Cut off excess fabric from underneath. Repeat on the other end of Red 7, being sure the diagonal is the opposite direction.
Repeat with Green "c" on both ends of Red 8.
Repeat with Green "c" on both ends of Red 9.

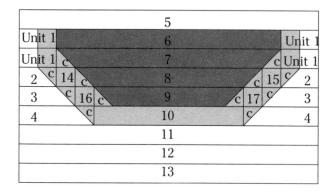

Row Assembly:
Row 2: Sew Unit 1- Red #6- Unit 1. Press.
Row 3: Sew Unit 1- Red #7- Unit 1. Press.
Row 4: Sew White #2- Green #14- Red #8- Green #15- White #2. Press.
Row 5: Sew White #3- Green #16- Red #9- Green #17- White #3. Press.
Row 6: Sew White #4- Green #10- White #4. Press.
Rows 7, 8 & 9: Sew 3 White strips #11-12-13 together. Press.
Rows 1 & 2: Sew 1 White strip #5 to Row #2. Press.
Sew the rows together. Press.

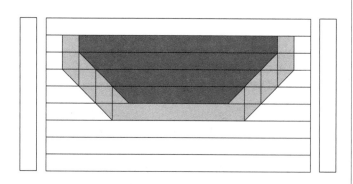

Borders:
Sew a White 9½"strip to each side of the block. Press.
The block will measure 9½" x 18½".
Make 3 Watermelon blocks.

Placemat

Refer to the Placemat Assembly diagram.
Use 1 Watermelon block.

BORDERS:

Top and Bottom:
Cut 2 Pink strips and 2 Aqua strips
18½" long.
Sew a Pink and Aqua strip together to
make a piece 2½" x 18½".
Repeat with the other 2 strips.
Sew a set to the top and bottom of
the mat. Press.

Sides:
Cut 2 White strips 13½" long for sides.
Sew side strips to the mat. Press.

Applique:
Refer to the Applique instructions.
For bird, cut 4 Aqua strips 6½" long.
Sew the strips together to make a piece
4½" x 6½". Press. Cut out 1 bird.
Applique bird to the Watermelon block.
For each beak, cut a 1" Yellow square and
fold into a beak shape.
Position under the bird and applique in place.
Embroider the eye with a French Knot.

July Watermelon and Bird Placemat Assembly

Quilting: See Basic Instructions.
Binding: Cut strips 2½" wide.
Sew together end to end to equal 76".
See Binding Instructions

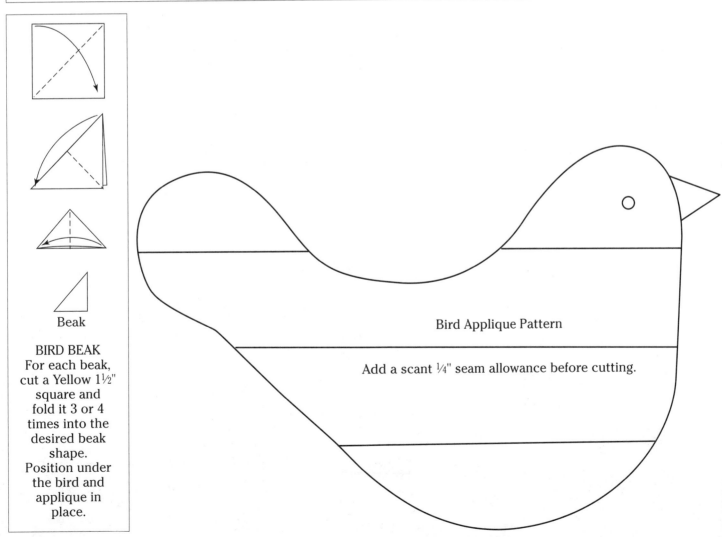

Beak

BIRD BEAK
For each beak,
cut a Yellow 1½"
square and
fold it 3 or 4
times into the
desired beak
shape.
Position under
the bird and
applique in
place.

Bird Applique Pattern

Add a scant ¼" seam allowance before cutting.

Table Runner

Refer to the Table Runner Assembly diagram.
Arrange all blocks on a work surface or table.
With the Pink sides touching, sew 2 rows of 2
    Block B's. Press.
Sew the rows together. Press.
Sew a Watermelon block on each end. Press.

Applique:

Refer to the Applique instructions.
For birds, cut 4 Aqua strips 13" long.
Sew the strips together to make a piece
    4½" x 13". Press.
Cut out 3 birds.
Applique a bird to each Watermelon block.
Use 2 birds for the Table Runnert.
For each beak, cut a 1" Yellow square and
    fold into a beak shape.
Position under the bird and applique in place.
Embroider the eye with a French Knot.

Rounded Ends:

Shape the ends of the runner into a curve.

Quilting: See Basic Instructions.
Binding: Cut strips 2½" wide.
    Sew together end to end to equal 134".
    See Binding Instructions.

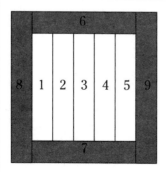

Potholder Block
Assembly

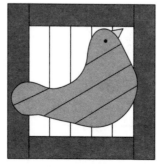

July Bird Potholder
Applique

Potholder

Cut 5 White strips 5½" long.
Sew the strips together to make a piece 5½" x 5½".
Borders:
    Cut 2 Red strips 5½" long for top and bottom.
    Cut 2 Red strips 7½" long for sides.
    Sew the top and bottom borders to the piece. Press.
    Sew the side borders to the piece. Press.

Applique: Refer to Placemat instructions and applique
    bird to a Potholder block.
Quilting: See Basic Instructions.
Binding: Cut 1 strip 2½" x 42".
    See Binding Instructions.

August – Homestead

Photo on page 11

SIZE: Table Runner: 14½" x 40"
          Placemat: 13" x 20"
          Potholders: 7" x 7"

YARDAGE:
We used a *Moda* "Legacy" by Howard Marcus
   'Honey Bun' collection of 1½" fabric strips
   - we purchased 1 'Honey Bun'

10 strips	OR	½ yard White
6 strips	OR	¼ yard Med Brown
4 strips	OR	⅙ yard Dark Brown
2 strips	OR	⅛ yard Tan/Cream
1 strip	OR	⅛ yard Med Blue
1 strip	OR	⅛ yard Red

Applique use a 4½" x 4½" scrap OR Purchase ⅛ yard Tan
Binding   Purchase ⅝ yard
Backing   Purchase 1 yard
Batting   Purchase 36" x 42"
Sewing machine, needle, thread

FABRIC FOR INDIVIDUAL PROJECTS:
Fabric or Scraps for Table Runner:

7 strips	OR	10½" x 44" of White (⅓ yard)
4 strips	OR	6" x 44" of Med Brown (⅙ yard)
3 strips	OR	4½" x 44" of Dk Brown (⅛ yard)
1 strip	OR	1½ x 44" of Blue
1 strip	OR	1½ x 44" of Red
Binding		Purchase 2½" x 110" (¼ yard)
Backing		Purchase ½ yard
Batting		Purchase 17" x 42"

Fabric or Scraps for Placemat:

3 strips	OR	4½" x 44" of White (⅛ yard)
2 strips	OR	3" x 44" of Tan
2 strips	OR	3" x 44" of Dark Brown
1 strip	OR	1½" x 44" of Med Brown
1 strip	OR	1½" x 44" of Blue
1 strip	OR	1½" x 44" of Red
Binding		Purchase 2½" x 76" (⅙ yard)
Backing		Purchase 15" x 22"
Batting		Purchase 15" x 22"

Scraps for Each Potholder:

1 strip	OR	1½" x 44" of each color
Binding		Purchase 2½" x 44" (⅛ yard)
Backing		Purchase 9" x 9"
Batting		Purchase 9" x 9"
Applique		4½" x 4½" of Tan

PREPARATION FOR STRIPS:
   Cut all strips 1½" by the width of fabric (usually 42" - 44").
   Label the stacks or pieces as you cut.

SEW BLOCKS:
   Refer to the Cutting Chart and Assembly instructions
     for each block. Label the pieces as you cut.

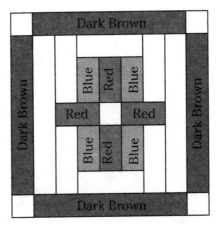

Block A - Assembly

For 2 of Block A:
CUTTING CHART:

	Quantity	Length	Position
Dark Brown	1	30"	Column A
	4	7½"	Top & Bottom borders
Red	1	10"	Unit C
	4	2½"	Center B (#3)
White	1	30"	Column A
	12	3½"	Unit C (#1 & #2)
	10	1½"	Center B (#4) and Cornerstones
Blue	2	10"	Unit C

PREPARATION FOR BLOCK A:
   Column A:
      Sew the 30" Dark Brown and White strips together. Press.
      Cut into 4 sections 2½" x 7½".
   Center B:
      Sew Red #3 - White #4 - Red #3.
      Make 2. Press.
   Unit C:
      Sew the 10" Blue - Red - Blue strips together. Press.
      Cut into 4 sections 2½" x 3½".
      Sew a White #1 to the top of each Unit C. Press.
      Sew a White #2 to the right and left sides of
         each Unit C. Press.

ASSEMBLE BLOCK A:
Sew Unit C to the top and
     bottom of Center B.
     Press.
     Make 2.

Sew a Column A to the right
     and left sides of
     each piece. Press.

Sew a White #4 cornerstone
     to each end of the
     Dark Brown border.
     Press.

Sew a border strip to the top
     and bottom of each
     block. Press.

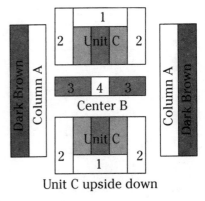

Unit C upside down

Block A Assembly

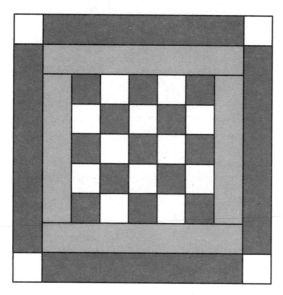

Block B - Assembly

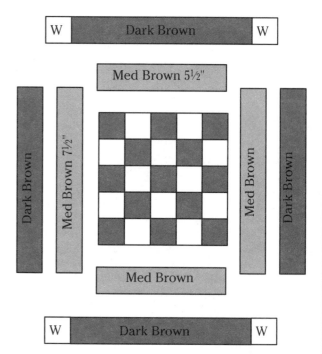

A - Row 1
B - Row 2
A - Row 3
B - Row 4
A - Row 5

Checkerboard
Assembly Diagram

Checkerboard:

Arrange the rows in the following order,
A - B - A - B - A.
Sew the rows together. Press.
Make 2.

For 2 of Block B:
CUTTING CHART:

	Quantity	Length	Position
Dark Brown	3	9"	Section A
	2	6"	Section B
White	2	9"	Section A
	3	6"	Section B
	4	1½"	Cornerstones
Medium Brown	4	7½"	Side border #1
	4	5½"	Top and Bottom border #1
Dark Brown	2	7½"	Top and Bottom border #2 on 1 block only
	2	7½"	Side border #2 on 1 block only

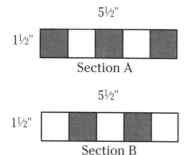

5½"

1½"

Section A

5½"

1½"

Section B

PREPARATION FOR BLOCK B
Section A for Rows 1, 3 & 5:
Sew 9" strips together side by side to make 5½" x 9":
Dk Brown - White - Dk Brown - White - Dk Brown.
Press.
Cut this piece into 6 sections 1½" x 5½". Label these "A".
Section B for Rows 2 & 4:
Sew 6" strips together side by side to make 5½" x 6":
White - Dk Brown - White - Dk Brown - White. Press.
Cut this piece into 4 sections 1½" x 5½". Label these "B".

| W | Dark Brown | W |

Med Brown 5½"

Dark Brown | Med Brown 7½" | Med Brown | Dark Brown

Med Brown

| W | Dark Brown | W |

Block B - Assembly Diagram

BLOCK ASSEMBLY:
Refer to the Block Assembly diagram.
Sew Med Brown 5½" strips to the top and bottom
of the block. Press.
Sew Med Brown 7½" strips to the left and right
sides of the block. Press.
Sew Dark Brown 7½" strips to the right and left
sides of 1 block. Press.
Sew a White 1½"cornerstone to each end of
remaining Dark Brown 7½" strips.
Press.
Sew strips to the top and bottom of 1 block. Press.

For 2 of BLOCK C:

Unit A - Corners:
Cut 2 White strips 20" long.
Sew the strips together to make
    a piece 2½" x 20".
Cut the strip into 8 units 2½" x 2½".

Unit A -
Corners

Unit B - Sides:
Cut 2 Med Brown strips 28" long.
Sew the strips together to make a
    piece 2½" x 28".
Cut the strip into 8 units 2½" x 3½".

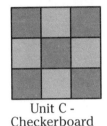

Unit B -
Sides

Border:
Cut 8 Dark Brown strips 7½" long.
Cut 8 White squares 1½" x 1½".

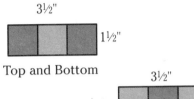

3½"

1½"

Top and Bottom

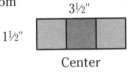

3½"

1½"

Center

Unit C -
Checkerboard

Unit C - Checkerboard Center:

Top and Bottom:
Cut 2 Red strips 1½" x 6". Cut 1 Blue strip 1½" x 6".
Sew the strips together Red-Blue-Red to make a
    piece 3½" x 6".
Cut into 4 sections 1½" x 3½".

Center:
Cut 2 Blue strips and 1 Red strip 3" long.
Sew the strips together Blue-Red-Blue to make a piece
    3" x 3½".
Cut into 2 sections 1½" x 3½".

Assemble Checkerboard:
Arrange the sections following the diagram.
Sew the sections together. Press.
Make 2.

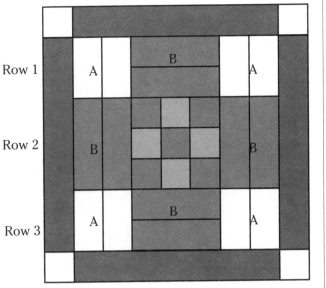

Row 1

Row 2

Row 3

Block C - Assembly Diagram

BLOCK C ASSEMBLY:
Follow the Block C Assembly Diagram.

Rows 1 & 3:
Sew a Unit A to each side of a Unit B. Press.

Row 2:
Sew a Unit B to each side of the checkerboard.
    Press.
Sew the rows together. Press.
Make 2 blocks.

Borders:
Sew a Dark Brown 7½" strip to the right and left
    sides of each block. Press.
Sew a White cornerstone to each end of the
    remaining Dark Brown strips. Press.
Sew a strip to the top and bottom of each block.
    Press.

For 2 of BLOCK D:

Cut 18 White strips 9½" long.
Sew 9 strips together to make
    a piece 9½" x 9½".
Press.
Make 2 blocks.

Cut on the Diagonal:
Draw a line on the diagonal
    from corner to corner and
    stay stitch ⅛" on both
    sides of line.
Cut along the diagonal line.

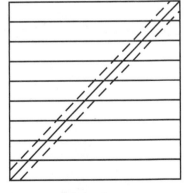

Block D
Sew 9 White strips together to
make a piece 9½" x 9½".

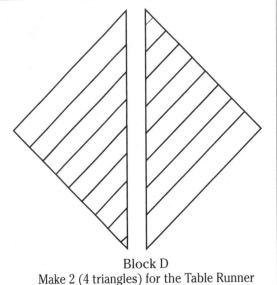

Block D
Make 2 (4 triangles) for the Table Runner

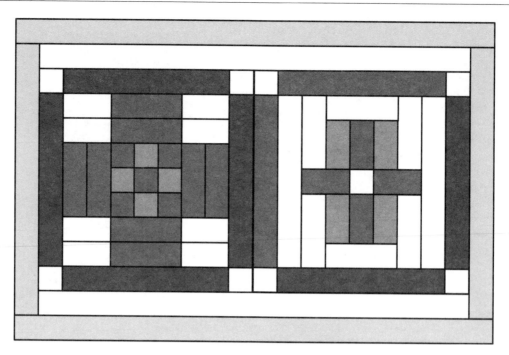

August Placemat Assembly Diagram

Placemat

Center: Sew a Block A to a Block C. Press.
Border #1: Cut 2 White strips 1½" x 18½".
    Sew the strips to the top and bottom of the mat.
      Press.
Border #2: Cut 2 Tan strips 1½" x 11½" for sides.

Cut 2 Tan strips 1½" x 20½" for top and bottom.
Sew the strips to the sides of the mat. Press.
Sew the strips to the top and bottom of the mat.
    Press.
Quilting: See Basic Instructions.
Binding: Cut strips 2½" wide.
    Sew together end to end to equal 76".
    See Binding Instructions.

Applique Swirl Potholder

Checkerboard Potholder

Potholders

Applique Swirl Potholder:
    Cut 5 Med Brown strips 5½" long.
    Sew the strips together. Press.
    Cut 2 White side borders 1½" x 5½".
    Sew borders to the piece. Press.
    Cut 2 White top/bottom borders 1½" x 7½".
    Sew borders to the piece. Press.
    Refer to the Applique Instructions.
    Cut out swirl pattern and applique as desired.
    Follow the instructions for Finishing Potholder.

Checkerboard Potholder:
    Omit the last border in the block instructions.
    Follow the instructions for Finishing Potholder.

FINISHING POTHOLDER:
Quilting: See Basic Instructions.
Binding: For each potholder, cut a strip
      2½" x 38".
    See Binding Instructions.

    Sew a loop in the upper left corner if desired.

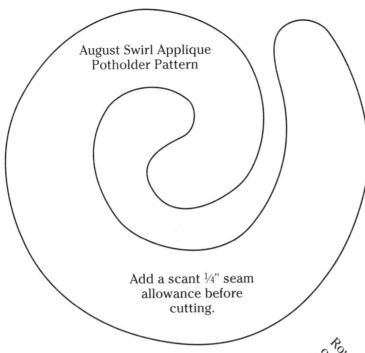

August Swirl Applique
Potholder Pattern

Add a scant ¼" seam
allowance before
cutting.

Table Runner

Refer to the Table Runner Assembly diagram.
Arrange all blocks on a work surface or table.

Row 1:
Sew a Block D to the left side of Block C. Press.

Row 2:
Sew a Block D to the left and right sides of Block B.
Press.

Row 3:
Sew a Block D to the right side of Block A.
Press.

Sew the rows together. Press.

Border:
Cut 2 Med Brown strips 9½". Label them #1 & 2.
Cut 2 Med Brown strips 10½". Label them #3 & 4.
Cut 2 Med Brown strips 29½". Label them #5 & 6.
Sew the borders to the runner in order. Press.
Because set-in triangles create an unusual fraction, we
have cut #5 & 6 longer than you need. Center and
trim to fit.

Quilting: See Basic Instructions.
Binding: Cut strips 2½" wide.
Sew together end to end to equal 110".
See Binding Instructions.

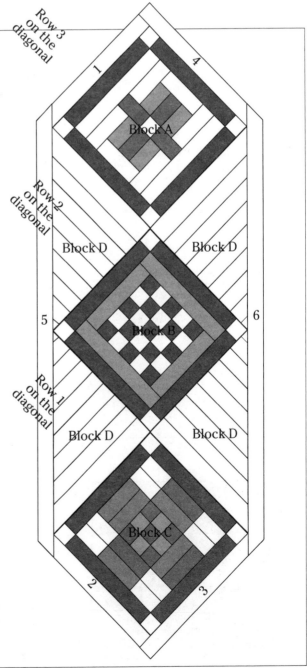

September – On the Farm

photo on page 12

SIZE: Table Runner: 17" x 42"
              Placemat: 12" x 17"
              Potholders: 7½" x 7½"

YARDAGE:
We used a *Moda* "Flag Day Farm" by Minick & Simpson
    'Honey Bun' collection of 1½" fabric strips
    - we purchased 1 'Honey Bun'

15 strips	OR	⅝ yard Tan/Ivory
6 strips	OR	¼ yard Red
6 strips	OR	¼ yard Navy
5 strips	OR	¼ yard Blue
Binding		Purchase ½ yard
Backing		Purchase 1 yard
Batting		Purchase 36" x 44"

Sewing machine, needle, thread

FABRIC FOR INDIVIDUAL PROJECTS:
Fabric or Scraps for Table Runner:

8 strips	OR	12" x 44" of Tan/Ivory (⅓ yard)
5 strips	OR	7½" x 44" of Red (¼ yard)
5 strips	OR	7½" x 44" of Navy (¼ yard)
4 strips	OR	6" x 44" of Blue (¼ yard)
Binding		2½" x 128" (⅓ yard)
Backing		½ yard
Batting		19" x 44"

Fabric or Scraps for Placemat:

6 strips	OR	9" x 44" of Tan/Ivory (¼ yard)
1 strip	OR	1½" x 44" of Red
1 strip	OR	1½" x 44" of Blue
1 strip	OR	1½" x 44" of Navy
Binding		2½" x 68" (⅙ yard)
Backing		14" x 19"
Batting		14" x 19"

Scraps for Each Potholder:

1 strip	OR	1½" x 44" of each color (⅛ yard)
Binding		2½" x 44" (⅛ yard)
Backing		9" x 9"
Batting		9" x 9"

PREPARATION FOR STRIPS:
    Cut all strips 1½" by the width of fabric
        (usually 42" - 44").

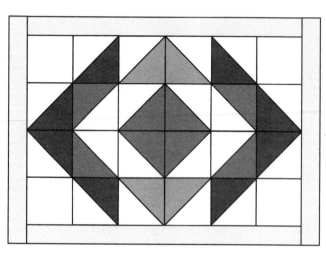

September Placemat Assembly Diagram

Placemat

Refer to the Placemat Assembly diagram.
Arrange all blocks on a work surface or table.
Assemble the rows following the diagram. Press.
Sew 4 rows of 6 blocks each. Press.
Sew the rows together. Press.

Borders:
    Cut 2 Tan/Ivory strips 15½" long for top and bottom.
    Cut 2 Tan/Ivory strips 12½" long for sides.
    Sew top and bottom strips to the mat. Press.
    Sew side strips to the mat. Press.

Quilting: See Basic Instructions.
Binding: Cut strips 2½" wide.
             Sew together end to end to equal 68".
             See Binding Instructions.

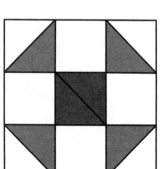

Potholder

Refer to the Potholder Assembly diagram.
Arrange all blocks on a work surface or table.
Assemble the rows following the diagram. Press.
Sew 3 rows of 3 blocks each. Press.
Sew the rows together. Press.

Quilting: See Basic Instructions.
Binding: Cut 1 strip 2½" x 42".
             See Binding Instructions.

September Table Runner Half Square Triangles

Navy/Red - Make 12

Navy/Ivory - Make 24

Navy/Blue - Make 8

Red/Ivory - Make 24

Red/Blue - Make 16

Blue/Ivory - Make 8

PREPARATION FOR HALF-SQUARE TRIANGLES:

Tan/Ivory Strips: Sew 3 strips together to make a piece
$3\frac{1}{2}$" x length of strip. Press.
Make 4 sets.
Also cut 3 strips $14\frac{1}{2}$" long and sew them together to
make a piece $3\frac{1}{2}$" x $14\frac{1}{2}$". Press.
Cut 52 squares $3\frac{1}{2}$" x $3\frac{1}{2}$".
Set aside 24 squares to use whole. (You will use 16 for the
table runner, 4 for the placemat, 4 for the potholder.)
Trim whole squares to 3" x 3".

Navy Strips: Sew 3 strips together to make a piece
$3\frac{1}{2}$" x length of strip. Press.
Make 2 sets.
Cut 22 squares $3\frac{1}{2}$" x $3\frac{1}{2}$" for the half-square triangles
and 1 square 3" x 3" for the potholder.

Blue Strips: Sew 3 strips together to make a piece
$3\frac{1}{2}$" x length of strip. Press.
Also cut 3 strips $14\frac{1}{2}$" long and sew them together to
make a piece $3\frac{1}{2}$" x $14\frac{1}{2}$". Press.
Cut 16 squares $3\frac{1}{2}$" x $3\frac{1}{2}$" for the half-square triangles.

Red Strips: Sew 3 strips together to make a piece
$3\frac{1}{2}$" x length of strip. Press. Make 2 sets.
Also cut 3 strips $7\frac{1}{2}$" long and sew them together to make
a piece $3\frac{1}{2}$" x $7\frac{1}{2}$". Press.
Cut 26 squares $3\frac{1}{2}$" x $3\frac{1}{2}$".

Match the following squares for the half-square triangles:
12 pairs of Red - Ivory/Tan
12 pairs of Navy - Ivory/Tan
4 pairs of Blue - Ivory/Tan
6 pairs of Navy - Red
4 pairs of Navy - Blue
8 pairs of Red - Blue

Follow the instructions in the Half-Square Triangle Diagram to
make 92 half-square triangles. Center and trim to 3" x 3".

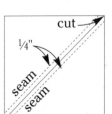

HALF-SQUARE TRIANGLES:
1. Place 2 squares right sides together.
2. Draw a diagonal line from corner to corner.
3. Stitch $\frac{1}{4}$" on each side of the line.
4. Cut squares apart on the diagonal line.
5. Open the 2 new squares with 2 colors.
6. Press. Trim off dog-ears.
7. Center and trim to size.

Table Runner

Refer to the Table Runner Assembly diagram.
Arrange all blocks on a work surface or table.
Assemble the rows following the diagram. Press.
Sew the rows together. Press.

BORDERS:

Sides: Cut 2 Tan/Ivory strips $25\frac{1}{2}$" long.
Label them #1-2.
Sew side strips to the runner. Press.

Ends: Cut 4 Tan/Ivory strips 13" long.
Label them #3-6.
Aligning the strip with the diagonals of the
squares center, pin and sew pieces
#3 & 4 to the runner.
Trim as needed. Press.
Center, pin and sew pieces #5 & 6 to the
runner. Trim as needed. Press.

Quilting: See Basic Instructions.
Binding: Cut strips $2\frac{1}{2}$" wide.
Sew together end to end to equal 128".
See Binding Instructions.

October – Pumpkins

photo on page 13

SIZE: Table Runner: 16" x 30"
        Placemat: 13" x 16"
        Potholders: 7" x 7"

YARDAGE:
We used a *Moda* "Fresh" by Deb Strain
  'Honey Bun' collection of 1½" fabric strips
  - we purchased 1 'Honey Bun'

6 strips	OR	⅓ yard Yellow
6 strips	OR	¼ yard Green
4 strips	OR	⅙ yard Orange
3 strips	OR	⅛ yard Blue
2 strips	OR	⅛ yard Red
2 strips	OR	⅛ yard White
2 strips	OR	⅛ yard Light Blue

Binding	Purchase ½ yard
Backing	Purchase ½ yard
Batting	Purchase 36" x 36"

Sewing machine, needle, thread
DMC pearl cotton or 6-ply floss
#22 or #24 chenille needle

FABRIC FOR INDIVIDUAL PROJECTS:

Fabric or Scraps for Table Runner:

5 strips	OR	7½" x 44" of Yellow (¼ yard)
3 strips	OR	4½" x 44" of Green (⅛ yard)
3 strips	OR	4½" x 44" of Orange (⅛ yard)
3 strips	OR	4½" x 44" of Blue (⅛ yard)
2 strips	OR	3" x 44" of White
1 strip	OR	1½" x 44" of Red
Binding	Purchase 2½" x 102" (¼ yard)	
Backing	Purchase ½ yard	
Batting	Purchase 18" x 32"	
Applique	Purchase 5½" x 12" of Black	

Fabric or Scraps for Placemat:

2 strips	OR	3" x 44" Light Blue
2 strips	OR	3" x 44" Green
1 strip	OR	1½" x 44" of Red
2 strips	OR	3" x 44" of Yellow
1 strip	OR	1½" x 44" of White
1 strip	OR	1½" x 44" of Orange
Binding	Purchase 2½" x 68" (⅙ yard)	
Backing	Purchase 15" x18"	
Batting	Purchase 15" x18"	
Applique	Purchase 4½" x 4½" Black, White, Yellow, Orange, Red	

Scraps for Each Potholder:

1 strip	OR	1½" x 44" of each color
Binding	Purchase 2½" x 44" (⅛ yard)	
Backing	Purchase 9" x 9"	
Batting	Purchase 9" x 9"	
Applique	Purchase 2½" x 3½" Black	

PREPARATION FOR STRIPS:
  Cut all strips 1½" by the width of fabric (usually
      42" - 44").

SEW BLOCKS:
  Refer to the Cutting Chart and Assembly instructions
      for each block.
  Label the pieces as you cut.

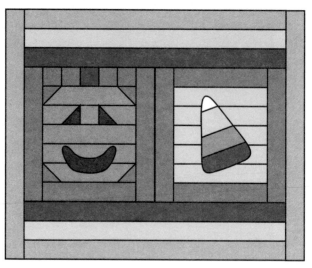

October Placemat Assembly

Placemat

Sew a Pumpkin Block A to a Candy Corn Block C.
Press.

Top and Bottom Borders:
  Cut 1 Red, 1 Yellow, and 1 Light Blue strip 29".
  Sew the strips together R-Y-B. Press.
  Cut the piece into 2 sections 3½" x 14½".
  Sew a strip to the top and bottom of the piece.
  Press.

Side Borders:
  Cut 2 Light Blue 13½" strips.
  Sew a strip to the left and right sides of the mat.
  Press.

Quilting: See Basic Instructions.
Binding: Cut strips 2½" wide.
  Sew together end to end to equal 68".
  See Binding Instructions.

Snowball Corners
  Several strips in each block use the
Snowball Corner technique. The direction of
the diagonal for each strip in the block varies,
so you must carefully note the diagonal on the
block assembly diagram. Some strips have a corner on only one end. The squares used as Corners
are labelled with a "c" in the cutting list.
  TIP: Fold back the triangle and check its
position before you sew.
  STEPS: Align a square with the appropriate
end of the strip and sew on the diagonal line. Fold
the triangle back, press before attaching it to any
other strips.

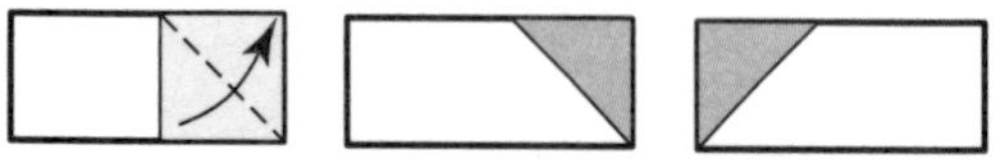

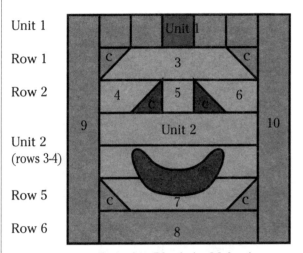

Unit 1

Row 1

Row 2

Unit 2
(rows 3-4)

Row 5

Row 6

Pumpkin Block A - Make 4

Sew Snowball Corners for the Eyes:
Line up a Black "c" on one end of #4.
Draw a diagonal line. Sew on the line. Fold corner back. Press.
Cut off excess fabric from underneath.
Repeat with Black "c" on #6.

Sew Green Corners to Strips 3 & 7:
Line up a Green "c" on one end of #3.
Draw a diagonal line. Sew on the line. Fold corner back. Press.
Cut off excess fabric from underneath.
Repeat on the other end of #3, being sure the
diagonal is in the opposite direction.
Repeat with Green "c" on both ends of #7.

Block Assembly:
   Row 3: Sew 4- 5- 6. Press.
   Refer to the Block A diagram. Arrange the pieces in rows.
   Sew the rows together. Press.
   Sew #9 & 10 to the left and right sides of the block. Press.
Applique: Refer to the Applique Instructions.
   Cut out 4 mouths using patterns.
   Applique as desired.

For 4 of Pumpkin Block A:
CUTTING CHART

	Quantity	Length	Position
Green	4	12"	Unit 1
	8	7½"	#9, 10
	4	5½"	#8
	16	1½"	#7c, #3c
Red	1	12"	Unit 1
Orange	2	22"	Unit 2
	8	5½"	#3, 7
	8	2½"	#4, 6
	4	1½"	#5
Black	8	1½"	Eyes #4c, #6c
	4	3½" x 8"	Mouth applique

5½"

1½"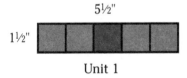

Unit 1

PUMPKIN BLOCK A ASSEMBLY:
Unit 1:
   Sew G-G-R-G-G to make a piece 5½" x 12". Press.
   Cut the piece into 8 units, each 1½" x 5½".
   Use 4 units for Row 1 of the Pumpkin block.

   Set aside 4 units for Row 3 of Block B.

5½"

2½"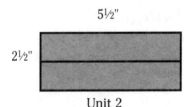

Unit 2

Unit 2:
   Sew 2 Orange strips together to make a piece
     2½" x 22". Press.
   Cut the piece into 4 units, each 2½" x 5½".

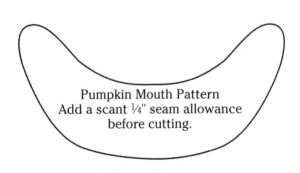

Pumpkin Mouth Pattern
Add a scant ¼" seam allowance
before cutting.

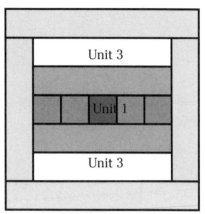

Block B - Make 4

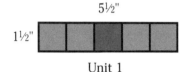

5½"

1½"

Unit 1

For 4 of Block B:

CUTTING CHART

Quantity	Length		Position
White	1	38½"	Unit 3
	1	5½"	Unit 3
Orange	1	38½"	Unit 3
	1	5½"	Unit 3
Yellow	8	5½"	Side borders
	8	7½"	Top and Bottom borders

BLOCK B ASSEMBLY:

Unit 1:

   Use 4 units you made in Block A.

Unit 3:

   Sew a 38½" White and Orange strip together to make a piece 2½" x 38½". Press.

   Cut the piece into 7 sections, each 2½" x 5½". Label these Unit 3.

   Sew the 5½" White and Orange strips together to make the eighth Unit 3. Press.

Block Assembly:

   Sew Unit 3 - Unit 1 - Unit 3. Press.

   Sew side borders to the block. Press.

   Sew top and bottom borders to the block. Press.

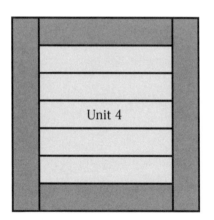

Block C for Applique
Make 3 for Candy Corn or Cat

For 3 of Block C:

CUTTING CHART

	Quantity	Length	Position
Green	2	16½"	Unit 4
	6	7½"	Side borders
Yellow	5	16½"	Unit 4
	1	5½"	Candy Corn applique
White	1	5½"	Candy Corn applique
Orange	1	5½"	Candy Corn applique
Red	1	5½"	Candy Corn applique
Black	2	5½" x 5½"	Cat appliques

BLOCK C ASSEMBLY:

Unit 4:

   Sew the Unit 4 strips together, Green - 5 Yellow - Green, to make a piece 7½" x 16½". Press.

   Cut the piece into 3 units 5½" x 7½".

   Refer to the Block C diagram.

   Sew a Green 7½" strip to the left and right sides of the block. Press.

Potholder Assembly

Pumpkin Potholder

Use a Pumpkin block.

Quilting: See Basic Instructions.
Binding: Cut 1 strip 2½" x 38".
See Binding Instructions.

Sew a loop to the upper left corner if desired.

Table Runner

Refer to the Table Runner Assembly diagram
and note the position of the pumpkins.
Arrange all blocks on a work surface or table.
Sew 2 rows of Blocks A-B-B-C. Press.
Sew the rows together. Press.

Border:
Cut 2 Blue strips 1½" x 28½" for sides.
Cut 2 Blue strips 1½" x 16½" for the ends.
Sew side borders to the runner. Press.
Sew end borders to the runner. Press.

Quilting: See Basic Instructions.
Binding: Cut strips 2½" wide.
Sew together end to end to equal 102".
See Binding Instructions.

Applique:
Refer to the Applique Instructions.
Sew the Candy Corn strips together,
White- Yellow-Orange- Red to make
a piece 4½" x 5½". Press.
Use this piece to cut out the Candy
corn applique.
Cut out 2 Black cats using patterns.
Applique as desired.
Make 2 blocks with cats for the Table
Runner and 1 block with Candy
corn for the placemat.

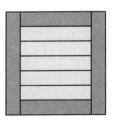

Use Block C
for Applique

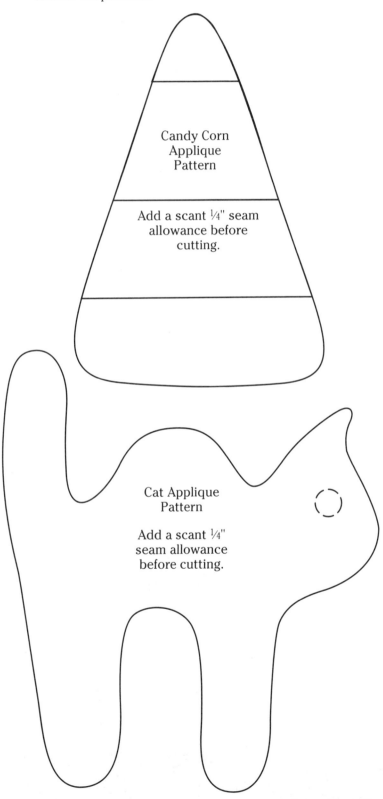

Candy Corn
Applique
Pattern

Add a scant ¼" seam
allowance before
cutting.

Cat Applique
Pattern

Add a scant ¼"
seam allowance
before cutting.

November – At Home

photo on page 14

SIZE: Table Runner: 20" x 38"
         Placemat: 13" x 20"
         Potholders: 7" x 7"

YARDAGE:
We used a *Moda* "Wildflower Serenade" by Kansas Troubles
    'Honey Bun' collection of 1½" fabric strips
    - we purchased 1 'Honey Bun'
    8 strips   OR   ⅓ yard Tan
    5 strips   OR   ¼ yard Red
    5 strips   OR   ¼ yard Green
    5 strips   OR   ¼ yard Navy
    4 strips   OR   ⅙ yard Black
    4 strips   OR   ⅙ yard Purple
    2 strips   OR   ⅛ yard Med Blue

Binding   Purchase ½ yard
Backing   Purchase 1 yard
Batting   Purchase 36" x 40"
Sewing machine, needle, thread

FABRIC FOR INDIVIDUAL PROJECTS:
Fabric or Scraps for Table Runner:
    6 strips   OR   9" x 44" of Tan (¼ yard)
    4 strips   OR   6" x 44" of Navy (⅙ yard)
    3 strips   OR   4½" x 44" of Black (⅛ yard)
    4 strips   OR   6" x 44" of Red (⅙ yard)
    3 strips   OR   4½" x 44" of Green (⅛ yard)
    3 strips   OR   4½" x 44" of Purple (⅛ yard)
    2 strips   OR   3" x 44" of Med Blue
    Binding   Purchase 2½" x 126" (¼ yard)
    Backing   Purchase ⅔ yard
    Batting   Purchase 22" x 40"
    Applique   included in the Red strips

Fabric or Scraps for Placemat:
    2 strips   OR   3" x 44" of Tan
    2 strips   OR   3" x 44" of Green
    1 strip   OR   1½" x 44" of Black
    1 strip   OR   1½" x 44" of Red
    1 strip   OR   1½" x 44" of Navy
    1 strip   OR   1½" x 44" of Purple
    1 strip   OR   1½" x 44" of Med Blue
    Binding   Purchase 2½" x 76" (⅙ yard)
    Backing   Purchase 15" x 22"
    Batting   Purchase 15" x 22"
    Applique   included in Red strips

Scraps for Each Potholder:
    1 strip   OR   1½" x 44" of each color
    Binding   Purchase 2½" x 44" of any color
    Backing   Purchase 9" x 9"
    Batting   Purchase 9" x 9"

PREPARATION FOR STRIPS:
    Cut all strips 1½" by the width of fabric (usually 42" - 44").
    Label the stacks or pieces as you cut.
SEW BLOCKS:
    Refer to the Cutting Chart and Assembly instructions for
each block. Label the pieces as you cut.

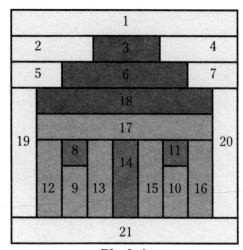

Block A
House

To Make 5 of Block A: House

CUTTING:
    Tan Sky:
        1, 21:   Cut 10 strips 1½" x 9½"
        2, 4:   Cut 10 strips 1½" x 3½"
        5, 7:   Cut 10 strips 1½" x 2½"
        19, 20:   Cut 10 strips 1½" x 5½"

    Black Roof:
        3:          Cut 5 strips 1½" x 3½"
        6:          Cut 5 strips 1½" x 5½"
        18:         Cut 5 strips 1½" x 7½"
    Red House:
        9, 10:   Cut 10 strips 1½" x 2½"
        12, 13, 15, 16:   Cut 20 strips 1½" x 3½"
        17:         Cut 5 strips 1½" x 7½"
    Navy Windows:
        8, 11:   Cut 10 squares 1½" x 1½"
    Navy Door:
        14:         Cut 5 strips 1½" x 3½"

ASSEMBLY:
    See Block Diagram.
Roof:
    Sew 2 to 3 to 4. Press.
    Sew 5 to 6 to 7. Press.
    Sew roof rows together. Press.

Window Sections:
    Sew 8 to 9. Press.
    Sew 10 to 11. Press.

House:
    Sew 12 to 8-9 to 13 to 14 to 15 to 10-11 to 16.
        Press.
    Sew 17 and 18 to the top. Press.
    Sew Tan sides 19 and 20. Press.
    Sew Tan strip 21 to the bottom. Press.
    Sew the Roof section to the House section.
        Press.

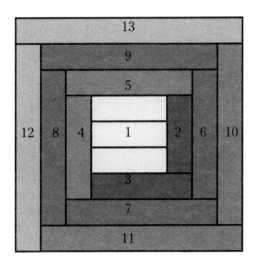

Block B - Log Cabin

To Make 5 of Block B: Log Cabin

Cutting:

1:	Cut 3 Tan 1½" x 21"
2:	Cut 5 Purple 1½" x 3½"
3:	Cut 5 Purple 1½" x 4½"
4:	Cut 5 Black 1½" x 4½"
5:	Cut 5 Black 1½" x 5½"
6:	Cut 5 Navy 1½" x 5½"
7 & 8:	Cut 10 Navy 1½" x 6½"
9:	Cut 5 Navy 1½" x 7½"
10:	Cut 5 Med Blue 1½" x 7½"
11:	Cut 5 Med Blue 1½" x 8½"
12:	Cut 5 Purple 1½" x 8½"
13:	Cut 5 Purple 1½" x 9½"
Applique	Cut 2 Red 1½" x 18"

Assembly:

Sew 3 Tan #1 strips together to make a
piece 3½" x 21". Press.

Cut 6 sections 3½" x 3½". Label these #1.
(Four sections are for the table runner; 1 for the
placemat. Set 1 aside for the heart potholder).

Sew Center square 1 to #2. Press.

Sew 1-2 to #3. Press. Sew 1-2-3 to #4. Press.

Continue adding strips in order, pressing
after each one, until all strips are complete.

Applique:

Refer to the Applique Instructions.

Sew 2 Red strips together to make a piece
2½" x 18". Cut out 6 hearts.

November Heart
Applique Pattern

Add a scant ¼" seam
allowance before
cutting.

Sew Tan strips
together for
center.
Applique heart.

Sew Purple
strips to the right
and
bottom of center.

Sew Navy strips
to the left and
top of center.

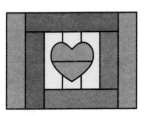 

Sew Red borders to
each side.

Sew Red borders to
top and bottom.

Heart Potholder

Center:

Use a Block B Tan center that you already made.

Cut 1 Purple strip 1½" x 3½".

Sew to the right side of the block.

Cut 1 Purple strip 4½"and sew to the bottom of the piece. Press.

Cut 1 Black strip 4½"and sew to the left side of the piece. Press.

Cut 1 Black strip 5½"and sew to the top of the piece. Press.

Border:

Cut 2 Red side borders 1½" x 5½".

Cut 2 Red top/bottom borders 1½" x 7½".

Sew side borders to the piece. Press.

Sew top and bottom borders to the piece. Press.

Quilting: See Basic Instructions.

Binding: Cut a strip 2½" x 42".
See Binding Instructions.

Sew a loop to the upper left corner if desired.

November Heart Potholder Assembly

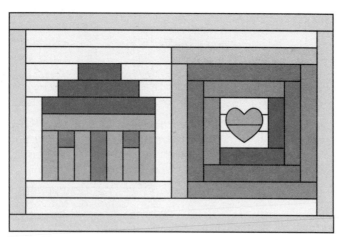

November Placemat Assembly

Placemat

Sew 1 heart block and 1 house block together.
   Press.
Cut 2 Tan strips 18½".
Sew a strip to the top and bottom of the mat.
   Press.

Border:
   Cut 2 Green strips 11½" long for sides.
   Cut 2 Green strips 20½" long for the top and bottom.
   Sew side borders to the mat. Press.
   Sew top and bottom borders to the mat. Press.

Quilting: See Basic Instructions.
Binding: Cut strips 2½" wide.
         Sew together end to end together to equal 76"
         See Binding Instructions.

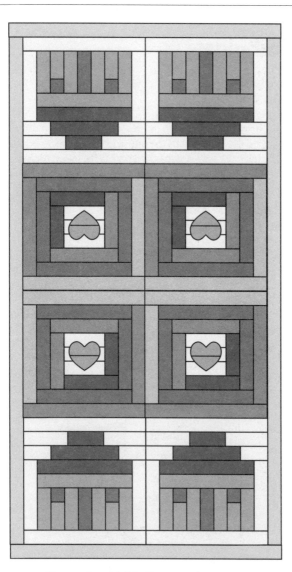

November Table Runner Assembly

Table Runner

Refer to the Table Runner Assembly diagram.
      Note the position of the hearts and houses.
   Arrange all blocks on a work surface or table.
   Sew 2 rows of House-Heart-Heart-House. Press.
   Sew the rows together. Press.

Border:
   Cut 2 Green strips 36½" long for sides.
   Cut 2 Green strips 20½" long for ends.
   Sew side borders to the runner. Press.
   Sew end borders to the runner. Press.

Quilting: See Basic Instructions.
Binding: Cut strips 2½" wide.
         Sew together end to end to equal 126".
         See Binding Instructions.

Potholder

Center:
Cut 5 Tan strips 5½" long. Sew the strips together. Press.

Border:
Cut 2 Green side borders 1½" x 5½".
Sew side borders to the piece. Press.
Cut 2 Green top/bottom borders 1½" x 7½".
Sew borders to the piece. Press.

Applique:
Cut 2 Red strips 3½" long.
Sew the strips together to make a piece 2½" x 3½". Press.
Use this piece to cut out the house body.
Cut 1 Navy strip 2½" long for door and window.
Cut 1 Black strip 4" long for roof and chimney.
Refer to the Applique Instructions. Applique as desired.

Quilting: See Basic Instructions.
Binding: Cut a strip 2½" x 42".
See Binding Instructions.

Sew a loop to the upper left corner if desired.

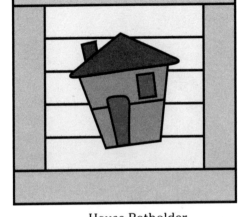

House Potholder

Sew 5 Tan strips together for center.

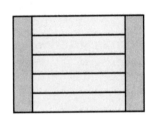

Sew Green side borders to center.

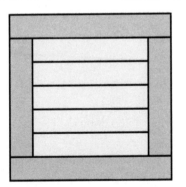

Sew Green top and bottom borders to center.

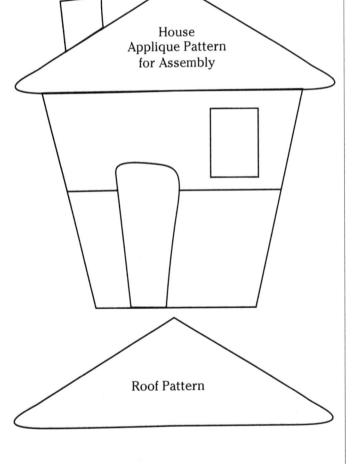

House
Applique Pattern
for Assembly

Roof Pattern

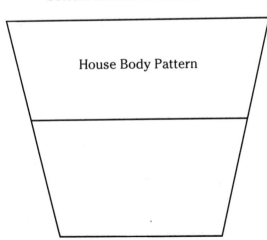

House Body Pattern

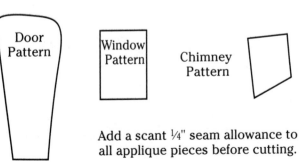

Door
Pattern

Window
Pattern

Chimney
Pattern

Add a scant ¼" seam allowance to
all applique pieces before cutting.

The Best Things About 'Honey Buns'

I love to quilt, but it is often difficult to find time to cut and piece a quilt top. When I saw collections of 1½" pre-cut fabric strips, I knew they were the answer.

No more spending hours choosing and cutting fabrics. Now I can begin sewing right away. Beautiful colors are available in every set. So whether I like jewel colors, heritage patterns, soft pastels or earthy tones... there is an assortment for me.

Now my goals... a handmade table runner for every table, beautiful placemats for each meal and a potholder for each of my children... are within reach. With 'Honey Buns' it is possible to complete a project in a weekend.

After I piece all the blocks together, I use leftover strips for the borders. Nothing really goes to waste and, if needed, I can purchase a bit of extra fabric for an extra punch of color or for the border and binding.

TIP: Quantities are given in strips and yardage so you know what you need and can start right away.

Tips for Working with Strips

Guide for Yardage:

1½" Strips - Each ¼ yard or a 'Fat Quarter' equals 6 strips - A pre-cut 'Honey Bun' strip is 1½" x 44"

Pre-cut strips are cut on the crosswise grain and are prone to stretching. These tips will help reduce stretching and make your quilt lay flat for quilting.

1. If you are cutting yardage, cut on the grain. Cut fat quarters on grain, parallel to the 18" side.

2. When sewing crosswise grain strips together, take care not to stretch the strips. If you detect any puckering as you go, rip out the seam and sew it again.

3. Press, Do Not Iron. Carefully open fabric, with the seam to one side, press without moving the iron. A back-and-forth ironing motion stretches the fabric.

4. Reduce the wiggle in your borders with this technique from garment making. First, accurately cut your borders to the exact measure of the quilt top. Then, before sewing the border to the quilt, run a double row of stay stitches along the outside edge to maintain the original shape and prevent stretching. Pin the border to the quilt, taking care not to stretch the quilt top to make it fit. Pinning reduces slipping and stretching.

Rotary Cutting

Rotary Cutter: Friend or Foe

A rotary cutter is wonderful and useful. When not used correctly, the sharp blade can be a dangerous tool. Follow these safety tips:

1. Never cut toward you.

2. Use a sharp blade. Pressing harder on a dull blade can cause the blade to jump the ruler and injure your fingers.

3. Always disengage the blade before the cutter leaves your hand, even if you intend to pick it up immediately.

Rotary cutters have been caught when lifting fabric, have fallen onto the floor and have cut fingers.

Basic Sewing

You now have precisely cut strips that are exactly the correct width. You are well on your way to blocks that fit together perfectly. Accurate sewing is the next important step.

Matching Edges:

1. Carefully line up the edges of your strips. Many times, if the underside is off a little, your seam will be off by ⅛". This does not sound like much until you have 8 seams in a block, each off by ⅛". Now your finished block is a whole inch wrong!

2. Pin the pieces together to prevent them shifting.

Seam Allowance:

I cannot stress enough the importance of accurate ¼" seams. All the quilts in this book are measured for ¼" seams unless otherwise indicated.

Most sewing machine manufacturers offer a Quarter-inch foot. A Quarter-inch foot is the most worthwhile investment you can make in your quilting.

Pressing:

I want to talk about pressing even before we get to sewing because proper pressing can make the difference between a quilt that wins a ribbon at the quilt show and one that does not.

Press, do NOT iron. What does that mean? Many of us want to move the iron back and forth along the seam. This "ironing" stretches the strip out of shape and creates errors that accumulate as the quilt is constructed. Believe it or not, there is a correct way to press your seams, and here it is:

1. Do NOT use steam with your iron. If you need a little water, spritz it on.

2. Place your fabric flat on the ironing board without opening the seam. Set a hot iron on the seam and count to 3. Lift the iron and move to the next position along the seam. Repeat until the entire seam is pressed. This sets and sinks the threads into the fabric.

3. Now, carefully lift the top strip and fold it away from you so the seam is on one side. Usually the seam is pressed toward the darker fabric, but often the direction of the seam is determined by the piecing requirements.

4. Press the seam open with your fingers. Add a little water or spray starch if it wants to close again. Lift the iron and place it on the seam. Count to 3. Lift the iron again and continue until the seam is pressed. Do NOT

use the tip of the iron to push the seam open. So many people do this and wonder later why their blocks are not fitting together.

5. Most critical of all: For accuracy every seam must be pressed before the next seam is sewn.

Working with 'Crosswise Grain' Strips:

Strips cut on the crosswise grain (from selvage to selvage) have problems similar to bias edges and are prone to stretching. To reduce stretching and make your quilt lay flat for quilting, keep these tips in mind.

1. Take care not to stretch the strips as you sew.

2. Adjust the sewing thread tension and the presser foot pressure if needed.

3. If you detect any puckering as you go, rip out the seam and sew it again. It is much easier to take out a seam now than to do it after the block is sewn.

Sewing Bias Edges:

Bias edges wiggle and stretch out of shape very easily. They are not recommended for beginners, but even a novice can accomplish bias edges if these techniques are employed.

1. Stabilize the bias edge with one of these methods:

   a) Press with spray starch.

   b) Press freezer paper or removable iron-on stabilizer to the back of the fabric.

   c) Sew a double row of stay stitches along the bias edge and ⅛" from the bias edge. This is a favorite technique of garment makers.

2. Pin, pin, pin! I know many of us dislike pinning, but when working with bias edges, pinning makes the difference between intersections that match and those that do not.

Building Better Borders:

Wiggly borders make a quilt very difficult to finish. However, wiggly borders can be avoided with these techniques.

1. Cut the borders on grain. That means cutting your strips parallel to the selvage edge.

2. Accurately cut your borders to the exact measure of the quilt.

3. If your borders are piece stripped from crosswise grain fabrics, press well with spray starch and sew a double row of stay stitches along the outside edge to maintain the original shape and prevent stretching.

4. Pin the border to the quilt, taking care not to stretch the quilt top to make it fit. Pinning reduces slipping and stretching.

Embroidery Use 24" lengths of doubled pearl cotton or 6-ply floss and a #22 or #24 Chenille needle (this needle has a large eye). Outline large elements.

Running Stitch Come up at A. Weave the needle through the fabric, making LONG stitches on the top and SHORT stitches on the bottom. Keep stitches even.

Applique Instructions

Basic Turned Edge

1. Trace pattern onto no-melt template plastic (or onto Wash-Away Tear-Away Stabilizer).

2. Cut out the fabric shape leaving a scant $1/4$" fabric border all around and clip the curves.

3. **Plastic Template Method** - Place plastic shape on the wrong side of the fabric. Spray edges with starch. Press a $1/4$" border over the edge of the template plastic with the tip of a hot iron. Press firmly.

4. **Stabilizer Method** - Place stabilizer shape on the wrong side of the fabric. Use a glue stick to press a $1/4$" border over the edge of the stabilizer securing it with the glue stick. Press firmly.

5. Remove the template, maintaining the folded edge on the back of the fabric.

6. Position the shape on the quilt and Blindstitch in place.

Basic Turned Edge by Hand

1. Cut out the shape leaving a $1/4$" fabric border all around.

2. Baste the shapes to the quilt, keeping the basting stitches away from the edge of the fabric.

3. Begin with all areas that are under other layers and work to the topmost layer.

4. For an area no more than 2" ahead of where you are working, trim to $1/8$" and clip the curves.

5. Using the needle, roll the edge under and sew tiny Blindstitches to secure.

Using Fusible Web for Iron-on Applique:

1. Trace pattern onto Steam a Seam 2 fusible web.

2. Press the patterns onto the wrong side of fabric.

3. Cut out patterns exactly on the drawn line.

4. Score web paper with a pin, then remove the paper.

5. Position the fabric, fusible side down, on the quilt. Press with a hot iron following the fusible web manufacturer's instructions.

6. Stitch around the edge by hand.

Optional: Stabilize the wrong side of the fabric with your favorite stabilizer.

Use a size 80 machine embroidery needle. Fill the bobbin with lightweight basting thread and thread machine with machine embroidery thread that complements the color being appliqued.

Set your machine for a Zigzag stitch and adjust the thread tension if needed. Use a scrap to experiment with different stitch widths and lengths until you find the one you like best.

Sew slowly.

Basic Layering Instructions

Marking Your Quilt:

If you choose to mark your quilt for hand or machine quilting, it is much easier to do so before layering. Press your quilt before you begin. Here are some handy tips regarding marking.

1. A disappearing pen may vanish before you finish.

2. Use a White pencil on dark fabrics.

3. If using a washable Blue pen, remember that pressing may make the pen permanent.

Pieced Backings:

1. Press the backing fabric before measuring.

2. If possible cut backing fabrics on grain, parallel to the selvage edges.

3. Piece 3 parts rather than 2 whenever possible, sewing 2 side borders to the center. This reduces stress on the pieced seam.

4. Backing and batting should extend at least 2" on each side of the quilt.

Creating a Quilt Sandwich:

1. Press the backing and top to remove all wrinkles.

2. Lay the backing wrong side up on the table.

3. Position the batting over the backing and smooth out all wrinkles.

4. Center the quilt top over the batting leaving a 2" border all around.

5. Pin the layers together with 2" safety pins positioned a handwidth apart. A grapefruit spoon makes inserting the pins easier. Leaving the pins open in the container speeds up the basting on the next quilt.

Basic Quilting Instructions

Hand Quilting:

Many quilters enjoy the serenity of hand quilting. Because the quilt is handled a great deal, it is important to securely baste the sandwich together. Place the quilt in a hoop and don't forget to hide your knots.

Machine Quilting:

All the quilts in this book were machine quilted. Some were quilted on a large, free-arm quilting machine and others were quilted on a sewing machine. If you have never machine quilted before, practice on some scraps first.

Straight Line Machine Quilting Tips:

1. Pin baste the layers securely.

2. Set up your sewing machine with a size 80 quilting needle and a walking foot.

3. Experimenting with the decorative stitches on your machine adds interest to your quilt. You do not have to quilt the entire piece with the same stitch. Variety is the spice of life, so have fun trying out stitches you have never used before as well as your favorite stand-bys.

Free Motion Machine Quilting Tips:

1. Pin baste the layers securely.

2. Set up your sewing machine with a spring needle, a quilting foot, and lower the feed dogs.

Basic Mitered Binding

A Perfect Finish:

The binding endures the most stress on a quilt and is usually the first thing to wear out. For this reason, we recommend using a double fold binding.

1. Trim the backing and batting even with the quilt edge.

2. If possible cut strips on the crosswise grain because a little bias in the binding is a Good thing. This is the only place in the quilt where bias is helpful, for it allows the binding to give as it is turned to the back and sewn in place.

3. Strips are usually cut 2½" wide, but check the instructions for your project before cutting.

4. Sew strips end to end to make a long strip sufficient to go all around the quilt plus 4"- 6".

5. With wrong sides together, fold the strip in half lengthwise. Press.

6. Stretch out your hand and place your little finger at the corner of the quilt top. Place the binding where your thumb touches the edge of the quilt. Aligning the edge of the quilt with the raw edges of the binding, pin the binding in place along the first side.

7. Leaving a 2" tail for later use, begin sewing the binding to the quilt with a ¼" seam.

For Mitered Corners:

1. Stop ¼" from the first corner. Leave the needle in the quilt and turn it 90°. Hit the reverse button on your machine and back off the quilt leaving the threads connected.

2. Fold the binding perpendicular to the side you sewed, making a 45° angle. Carefully maintaining the first fold, bring the binding back along the edge to be sewn.

3. Carefully align the edges of the binding with the quilt edge and sew as you did the first side. Repeat this process until you reach the tail left at the beginning. Fold the tail out of the way and sew until you are ¼" from the beginning stitches.

4. Remove the quilt from the machine. Fold the quilt out of the way and match the binding tails together. Carefully sew the binding tails with a ¼" seam. You can do this by hand if you prefer.

Finishing the Binding:

5. Trim the seam to reduce bulk.

6. Finish stitching the binding to the quilt across the join you just sewed.

7. Turn the binding to the back of the quilt. To reduce bulk at the corners, fold the miter in the opposite direction from which it was folded on the front.

8. Hand-sew a Blind stitch on the back of the quilt to secure the binding in place.

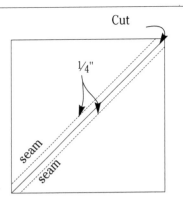

Half-Square Triangle
1. Place 2 squares right sides together.
2. Draw a diagonal line from corner to corner.
3. Stitch ¼" on each side of the line.
4. Cut squares apart on the diagonal line.
5. Open the 2 new squares with 2 colors.
6. Press. Trim off dog-ears.
7. Center and trim to size.

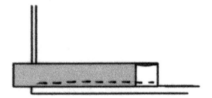

Align the raw edge of the binding with the raw edge of the quilt top. Start about 8" from the corner and go along the first side with a ¼" seam.

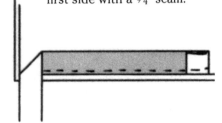

Stop ¼" from the edge. Then stitch a slant to the corner (through both layers of binding)... lift up, then down, as you line up the edge. Fold the binding back.

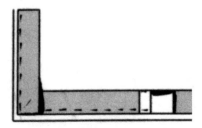

Align the raw edge again. Continue stitching the next side with a ¼" seam as you sew the binding in place.

December – Favorite Things

photo on page 15

SIZE: Table Runner: 16" x 28"
              Placemat: 13" x 18"
              Potholders: 7" x 7"

YARDAGE:
We used a *Moda* "Harmony" by Jan Patek
    'Honey Bun' collection of 1½" fabric strips
    - we purchased 1 'Honey Bun'

8 strips	OR	⅓ yard Red
7 strips	OR	⅓ yard Tan/Cream
7 strips	OR	⅓ yard Green
4 strips	OR	⅙ yard Black
4 strips	OR	⅙ yard Med Tan
2 strips	OR	⅛ yard Blue
1 strip	OR	⅛ yard Paisley

Binding   Purchase 1 yard
Backing   Purchase 1 yard
Batting   Purchase 36" x 36"
Sewing machine, needle, thread
DMC pearl cotton or 6-ply floss
#22 or #24 chenille needle

PREPARATION FOR STRIPS:
    Cut all strips 1½" by the width of fabric (usually 42" - 44").
    Label the stacks or pieces as you cut.

SEW BLOCKS:
    Refer to the Cutting Chart and Assembly instructions for
       each block. Label the pieces as you cut.

FABRIC FOR INDIVIDUAL PROJECTS:

Fabric or Scraps for Table Runner:

5 strips	OR	7½" x 44" of Red (¼ yard)
3 strips	OR	4½" x 44" of Black (⅛ yard)
3 strips	OR	4½" x 44" of Tan/Cream (⅛ yard)
3 strips	OR	4½" x 44" of Green (⅛ yard)
2 strips	OR	3" x 44" of Med Tan
1 strip	OR	1½" x 44" of Blue
1 strip	OR	1½" x 44" of Paisley
Binding		Purchase 2½" x 98" (¼ yard)
Backing		Purchase ½ yard
Batting		Purchase 18" x 30"

Fabric or Scraps for Placemat:

3 strips	OR	4½" x 44" of Green (⅛ yard)
2 strips	OR	3" x 44" of Med Tan
2 strips	OR	3" x 44" of Tan/Cream
1 strip	OR	1½" x 44" of Red
Binding		Purchase 2½" x 72" (⅙ yard)
Backing		Purchase 15" x 20"
Batting		Purchase 15" x 20"

Scraps for 6 Potholders:

3 strips	OR	4½" x 44" of Green (⅛ yard)
3 strips	OR	4½" x 44" of Black (⅛ yard)
3 strips	OR	4½" x 44" of Tan/Cream (⅛ yard)
3 strips	OR	4½" x 44" of Red (⅛ yard)
1 strip	OR	1½" x 44" of Blue
1 strip	OR	1½" x 44" of Paisley
2 strips	OR	3" x 44" of Med Tan
Binding		Purchase 2½" x 44" for each potholder
Backing		Purchase 9" x 9" for each potholder6
Batting		Purchase 9" x 9" for each potholder

For 2 of Bird Block 1:

CUTTING
- Cut 5 Black strips 11" long for the center.
- Cut 4 Blue strips 5½" long for the side borders.
- Cut 4 Blue strips 7½" long for the top and bottom borders.
- Cut 4 Red strips 8" long for bird applique.
- Cut 1 Tan strip 2" long for beak applique.

December Block 1 Assembly

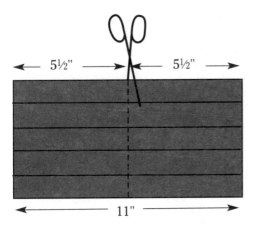

Sew 5 Black strips together. Press.

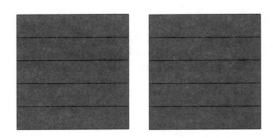

Cut the piece into 2 squares, each 5½" x 5½".

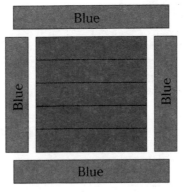

Block 1 - Assembly Diagram

ASSEMBLE BLOCK 1:
Sew 5½" Blue strips to the right and left sides of the block. Press.
Sew 7½" Blue strips to the top and bottom of the block. Press.

APPLIQUE:
Sew 4 Red strips together. Press.
Use this piece to cut out 2 birds.
To make the beak, cut a 1" square and fold into a beak shape as shown in the diagram
Refer to the Applique instructions.
Applique as desired.
Embroider the eye with a French Knot.

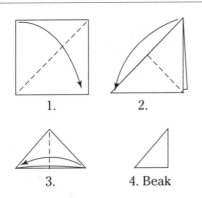

1.   2.

3.   4. Beak

BIRD BEAK
For each beak, cut a Tan 1½" square and fold it 3 or 4 times into the desired beak shape.
Position under the bird and applique in place.

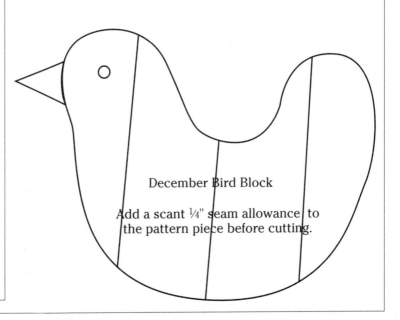

December Bird Block

Add a scant ¼" seam allowance to the pattern piece before cutting.

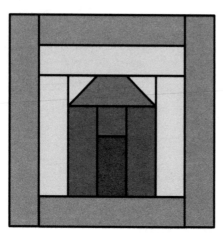

Block 2 - Assembly Diagram

For 2 of House Block 2:

CUTTING CHART

	Quantity	Length	Position
Black	2	2½"	#2
Blue	2	1½"	#1
	4	3½"	#3, 4
Red	2	3½"	#5
Tan	4	1½	#5 "c"
	4	4½"	#6, 7
	2	5½"	#8
Green	4	5½"	#9, 10
	4	7½"	#11, 12

ASSEMBLE BLOCK 2:

Sew #1-2. Press
Sew #3 & 4 to the left and right sides of the block. Press.
Align 1 Tan "c" square on each end of #5.
Refer to the Snowball Corner instructions.
Sew on the diagonal, fold back the pieces and press.
Sew #5 to the top of the block. Press.
Sew #6 & 7 to the left and right sides of the block. Press.
Sew #8 & 9 to the top of the block. Press.
Sew #10 to the bottom of the block. Press.
Sew #11 & 12 to the left and right sides of the block. Press.

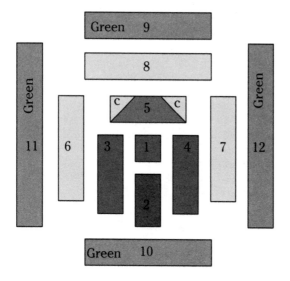

Block 2 - Assembly Diagram

Snowball Corners

Several strips in each block use the Snowball Corner technique. The direction of the diagonal for each strip in the block varies, so you must carefully note the diagonal on the block assembly diagram. Some strips have a corner on only one end. The squares used as Corners are labelled with a "c" in the cutting list.

TIP: Fold back the triangle and check its position before you sew.

STEPS: Align a square with the appropriate end of the strip and sew on the diagonal line. Fold the triangle back, press before attaching it to any other strips.

For 2 of Block 3:

CUTTING
Cut 4 Med Tan strips 5½" long for the side borders.
Cut 4 Med Tan strips 7½" long for the top and bottom borders.
Cut 3 Green and 3 Red strips 14" long for pinwheels.

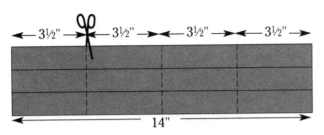

Sew 3 Green strips. Cut 4 sections 3½" x 3½".
Repeat for 3 Red strips.

PREPARATION FOR BLOCK 3
Sew 3 Green strips together to make a piece 3½" x 14".
Cut the piece in 4 squares 3½" x 3½".
Repeat for the Red strips.
Refer to the Half-Square Triangle instructions on page 59.
Match up 4 pairs of Red-Green squares to make 8 half-square triangles.

Each pair of Red/Green squares
makes 2 Half-Square Triangle blocks.

Trim each block
to 3" x 3".

ASSEMBLE A PINWHEEL:
Arrange 4 half-square triangles in
a Pinwheel.
TIP: It is not necessary to match
the interior seams.
Sew 2 rows of 2 blocks. Press.
Sew the rows together. Press.

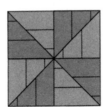

Pinwheel Block

Block 3

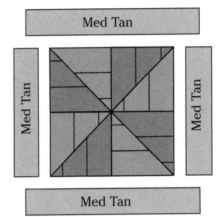

Block 3 - Assembly Diagram

ASSEMBLE BLOCK 3:
Sew 5½" Med Tan strips to the right
and left sides of the block. Press.
Sew 7½" Med Tan strips to the top
and bottom of the block. Press.

For 2 of Block 4: Log Cabin

CUTTING
1:	Cut 2 Red 1½" x 1½"
2:	Cut 2 Red 1½" x 1½"
3, 4	Cut 4 Green 1½" x 2½"
5, 6:	Cut 4 Red 1½" x 3½"
7, 8:	Cut 4 Green 1½" x 4½"
9:	Cut 2 Red 1½" x 5½"
10, 11:	Cut 4 Med Tan 1½" x 5½"
12, 13:	Cut 4 Med Tan 1½" x 7½"

SEW BLOCKS
Sew #1 to #2. Press.
Sew 1-2 to #3. Press.
Sew 1-2-3 to #4. Press.
Sew 1-2-3-4 to #5. Press.
Continue adding strips in order. Press.

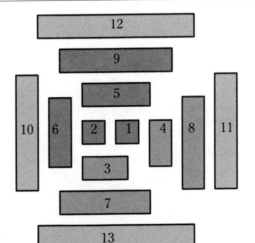

Block 4 Assembly Diagram

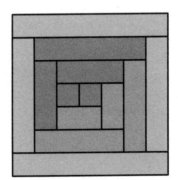

Block 4 Assembly

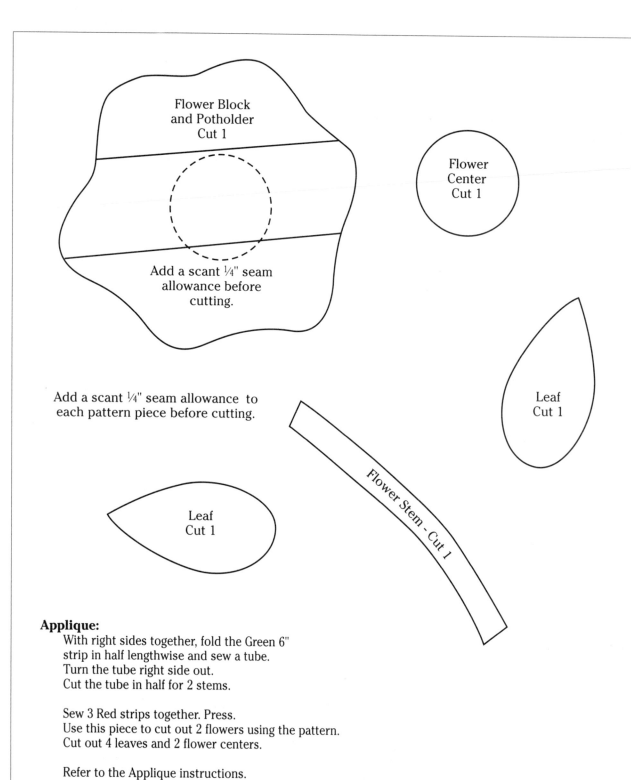

**Flower Block
and Potholder
Cut 1**

Add a scant ¼" seam
allowance before
cutting.

**Flower
Center
Cut 1**

**Leaf
Cut 1**

Add a scant ¼" seam allowance to
each pattern piece before cutting.

**Leaf
Cut 1**

Flower Stem - Cut 1

Applique:
  With right sides together, fold the Green 6"
  strip in half lengthwise and sew a tube.
  Turn the tube right side out.
  Cut the tube in half for 2 stems.

  Sew 3 Red strips together. Press.
  Use this piece to cut out 2 flowers using the pattern.
  Cut out 4 leaves and 2 flower centers.

  Refer to the Applique instructions.
  Applique as desired.

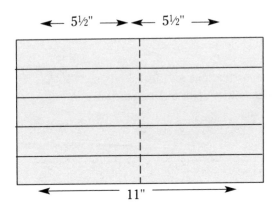

Sew 5 Tan strips together. Press.
Cut 2 squares 5½" x 5½".

ASSEMBLE BLOCK 5:

Center:

Sew 5 Tan strips together. Press.
Cut 2 squares 5½" x 5½".

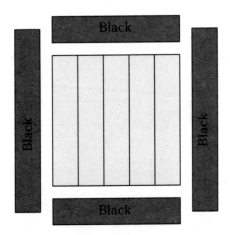

Block 5 - Assembly Diagram

Sew 5½" Black strips to the top and bottom
of the block. Press.
Sew 7½" Black strips to the right and left sides
of the block. Press.

For 2 of Flower Block 5:

CUTTING

Cut 5 Tan strips 11" long for the center.
Cut 4 Black strips 5½" long for the top and
bottom borders.
Cut 4 Black strips 7½" long for the side borders
Cut 3 Red strips 7" long for flower applique.
Cut 1 Green strip 8" long for leaves.
Cut 1 Green strip 6" long for stems.

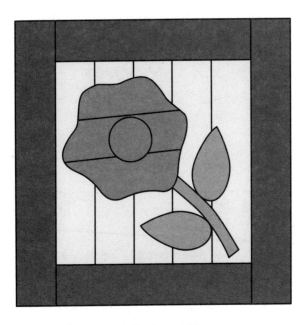

Block 5 - Assembly

Block 6 - Assembly
with Doll Applique

For 2 of Girl Block 6:

CUTTING
Cut 5 Tan strips 11" long for the center.
Cut 4 Med Tan strips 5½" long for the side borders.
Cut 4 Med Tan strips 7½" long for the top and bottom borders.
Cut 3 Red strips 7" long for dress applique.
Cut 1 Med Tan strip 3" long for head.

ASSEMBLE BLOCK 6:

Center:
Follow the instructions for Block 5 on page 77.
Change the border color to Medium Tan.

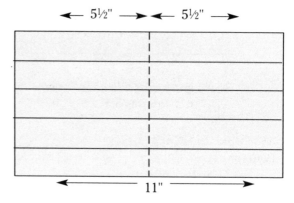

Sew 5 Tan strips together. Press.
Cut 2 squares 5½" x 5½".

Head

Girl Dress
Pattern

Add a scant ¼" seam
allowance before
cutting.

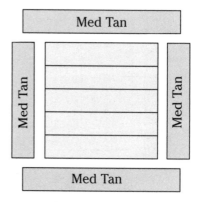

Block 6 - Borders

Applique:
Sew 3 Red strips together. Press.
Use this piece to cut out 2 dresses using the pattern.
Cut out 2 heads from Medium Tan.

Refer to the Applique instructions.
Applique as desired.
Embroider the eyes with a French Knot.
Embroider the hair, hands and legs with a Straight stitch.
Embroider the mouth with a Stem Stitch.

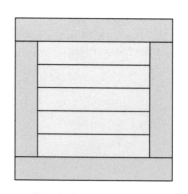

Block 6 - Assembly

For 2 of Mistletoe Block 7:

CUTTING
- Cut 5 Black strips 11" long for the center.
- Cut 4 Paisley strips 5½" long for the top and bottom borders.
- Cut 4 Paisley strips 7½" long for the side borders.
- Cut 3 Green strips 14" long for leaf applique.
- Cut 1 Red strip 9" long for berries.

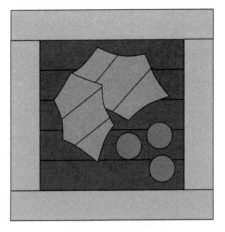

Block 7 - Assembly

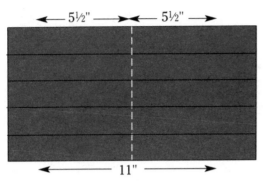

Sew 5 Black strips together. Press.
Cut 2 squares 5½" x 5½".

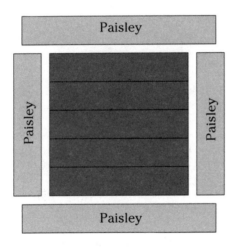

Block 7 - Assembly Diagram

ASSEMBLE BLOCK 7:

Center:
Sew 5 Black strips together. Press. Cut 2 squares 5½" x 5½".
Sew 5½" Paisley strips to the left and right sides of the block. Press.
Sew 7½" Paisley strips to the top and bottom of the block. Press.

Applique:
Sew 3 Green strips together.
Press.
Use this piece to cut out
4 leaves using the pattern.
Refer to the Applique
instructions.
Applique as desired.

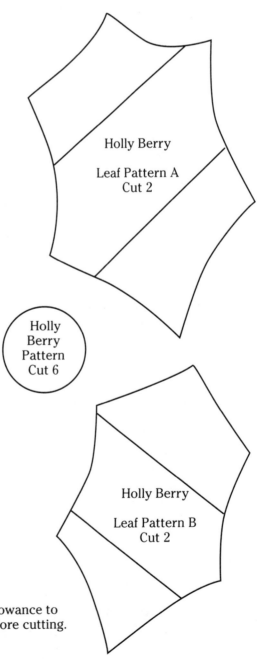

Holly Berry
Leaf Pattern A
Cut 2

Holly Berry Pattern Cut 6

Holly Berry
Leaf Pattern B
Cut 2

Add a scant ¼" seam allowance to each applique pattern before cutting.

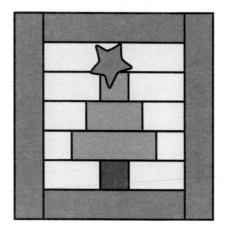

December Block 8
Assembly
with Applique

For 2 of Tree Block 8:

CUTTING CHART

	Quantity	Length	Position
Tan	8	2½"	#1, 3, 10, 12
	4	1½"	#4, 6
	4	2"	#7, 9
	2	5½"	#13
Black	2	1½"	#2
Red	4	5½"	#14, 15
	4	7½"	#16, 17
	1	4"	Star applique
Green	2	3½"	#5
	2	2½"	#8
	2	1½"	#11

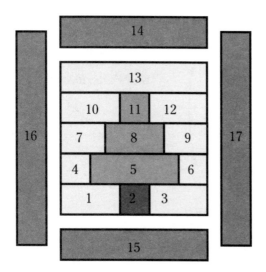

December Block 8 Assembly

ASSEMBLE BLOCK 8:

Center:
Row 1: Sew #1-2-3. Press
Row 2: Sew #4-5-6. Press.
Row 3: Sew #7-8-9. Press.
Row 4: Sew #10-11-12. Press.
Sew the rows together. Press.
Sew #13 & 14 to the top of the piece. Press.
Sew #15 to the bottom of the piece. Press.
Sew #16 & 17 to the left and right sides of the block.
   Press.

Applique:
Cut out 2 stars using the pattern.
Refer to the Applique instructions.
Applique as desired.

December
Christmas
Tree Star
Pattern

Add a scant ¼" seam
allowance before
cutting.

Block 1 - Bird Potholder

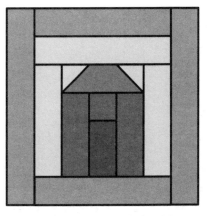

Block 2 - House Potholder

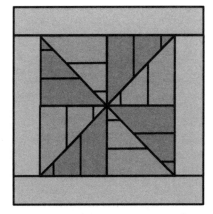

Block 3 Pinwheel Potholder

Block 4 Log Cabin Potholder

Block 5 - Flower Potholder

Block 6 - Girl Potholder

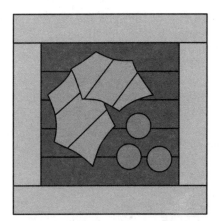

Block 7 - Holly Potholder

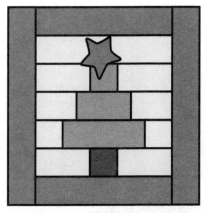

Block 8 - Tree Potholder

Potholders

Make a potholder from any block.

Quilting: See Basic Instructions.
Binding: Cut a strip 2½" x 42".
         See Binding Instructions.

         Sew a loop to the upper
            left corner if desired.

December Table Runner Assembly

Table Runner

Arrange all blocks on a work surface or table.
Sew 2 rows of 4 blocks each. Press.
Sew the rows together. Press.

Borders:
Cut 2 Red strips 28½" long for the sides.
Cut 2 Red strips 16½" long for the ends.
Sew the sides to the table runner. Press.
Sew the ends to the table runner. Press.

Quilting: See Basic Instructions.
Binding: Cut strips 2½" wide.
Sew together end to end to equal 98".
See Binding Instructions.

SUPPLIERS

Most quilt and fabric stores carry an excellent assortment of supplies. If you need something special, ask your local store to contact the following companies.

"HONEY BUNS" FABRIC ROLLS
MODA fabrics, United Notions, Dallas, TX

QUILTING BY
Susan Corbett, 817-361-7762
Julie Lawson, 817-428-5929
Sue Needle, 817-589-1168

MANY THANKS to my staff for their cheerful help and wonderful ideas!
Kathy Mason • Patty Williams • Donna Kinsey
Kristy Krouse • David & Donna Thomason

December Placemat Assembly

Placemat

Sew Block 3 to Block 4. Press.

Border #1:
Cut 2 Tan/Cream strips 14½" long for the top and bottom.
Cut 2 Tan/Cream strips 9½" long for the sides.
Sew the top and bottom strips to the mat. Press.
Sew the sides to the mat. Press.

Border #2:
Cut 2 Tan/Cream strips 16½" long for the top and bottom.
Sew the top and bottom strips to the mat. Press.

Border #3:
Cut 2 Green strips 11½" long for the sides.
Cut 2 Green strips 18½" long for the top and bottom.
Sew the sides to the mat. Press.
Sew the top and bottom strips to the mat. Press.

Quilting: See Basic Instructions.
Binding: Cut strips 2½" wide.
Sew together end to end to equal 72".
See Binding Instructions.